SuperWoman Redefined:
Why Being Independent is Overrated

by Ashley Hence, LPC-S, CRC, NCC

To: Vanessa
Thank you for supporting me. I hope you enjoy and I can't wait to hear your feedback

SuperWoman Redefined: Why Being Independent is Overrated

Copyright © 2019 by UImpact Publishing Group

All Rights Reserved

No part of this book may be used, reproduced, uploaded, stored or introduced into a retrieval system, or transmitted in any way or by any means (including electronic, mechanical, recording, or otherwise), without the prior written permission of the publisher, with the exception of brief quotations for written reviews or articles. No copying, uploading, or distribution of this book via the Internet is permissible.

The author, writers, and publisher have made every effort to include accurate information and website addresses in this work at the time of publication, and assume no responsibility for changes, omissions, inaccuracies, or errors that occur before or after publication. The publisher does not endorse or assume responsibility for information, author and writer websites, or third-party websites, or their content.

SuperWoman Redefined: Why Being Independent is Overrated

ISBN: 9781795754729

Hey, you, superwoman! Yes, *you*. I think your cape is a little dirty! Perhaps it's time to take it to the dry cleaners. You've been clocking overtime, working hard, getting so much use out of that uniform. It just might be time to take that costume off and clean it, maybe spray a little Febreze on it. Instead of driving that save the world superhero car, let's switch it up and you can just hop in the passenger seat while I drive for a second. Buckle up-it's "go time!"

I've previously had random conversations with my friends and family about life, and one of them mentioned that other people just seem to "have it all together." This made me think *Well, I don't*.

Whenever I say that, the person I'm speaking to always says, "Well, you always seem like you do." This made me think *if only you knew what's really going on behind the smile*. It also made me wonder how many other women have so much going on, but just aren't comfortable enough to be transparent, shed their independent "I can do it all" cape, and let the world know: "Hey, I'm struggling over here!" That's what sparked the idea for this book. I want to speak to the modern-day woman to discuss the thoughts, fears, doubts, questions, and day-to-day activities she doesn't talk about due to fear of being judged. I hope you can relate to something in this book and that it will inspire you to start a dialogue about how to get help with this thing called life. I also hope it helps you better understand the importance of self-care. And I hope to encourage you to recognize your *badazzness*. Enjoy.

Acknowledgments

Wow, I really can't believe I finished this book! I remember not wanting to write at all. You are probably wondering why. Well, it's because I didn't think I had that much to say. It's hard to tell with so many chapters, but I had to take some of my own advice and believe in myself. God really showed out by blessing me to have wonderful people in my life who kept me motivated.

I really want to thank so many, but the first person that comes to mind is my sister, Shania (my best friend in the whole wide world. She really stayed on my last nerve about writing a book. She believed in me when I didn't believe in myself. She would not stop talking to me about it to the point where I was annoyed and thinking, *Why do you keep talking to me about something that I am telling you I'm not cut out to do?* I'm glad she did, because she motivated me to try something outside of my comfort zone. She never ceases to amaze me, and I'm so blessed to have her as my big sister and biggest supporter. I love you, Sissy.

Next is my friend, Alexandria. Once I told her how much my sister was getting on my nerves about the idea of writing a book, she picked up where my sister left off in annoying me to get started. Just when I thought I was getting some relief, she confirmed that I needed to get off my butt and do it. Thanks, NB.

To Toni my ultimate shero. Your strength amazes me and I'm so glad to call you my bestie. Also, my Aunt Pat has been so helpful in giving me tips as well. Thank you to my friend, Greg, for telling me how to self-publish, for being the first one to make me read my rough draft out loud to him, and for offering supportive feedback. Talk about nervousness. Thank you soror Alex for giving me first time writer tips and helping me ease my anxiety on putting my info out to the world. "Now keep in mind that I'm an artist, and I'm sensitive about my ish," lol. But here it is, my first book-and if I only sell one copy it doesn't matter. I'm just so proud that I finished what I started. I appreciate all my friends, family, sorors, and clients for their support, listening ears, and encouragement.

Table of Contents

Chapter 1:
Your Boundaries Should be Higher Than Trump's Ego!............ 10

Chapter 2:
Is Your Oxygen Mask Secure Before You Help Put on Your Neighbor's?..14

Chapter 3:
Is Your Happy Meter Broken?..18

Chapter 4:
How Many Dependents Are You Claiming on Those Taxes?.......23

Chapter 5:
Me Time: I'm Lonely, But Shhh, Don't Tell Anyone……………...29

Chapter 6:
Feelings, All in My Feelings…………………………………...…..34

Chapter 7:
Your Healing Is Your Responsibility……………………………….38

Chapter 8:
I Thought Therapy Was for Crazy People (which I'm not)!..........42

Chapter 9:
Do Not Disturb-Block Is Your Best Friend……………….………..45

Chapter 10:
Limit Your "Clap Backs," Sis..48

Chapter 11:
Viewer's Choice..51

Chapter 12:
The Original Cannot Be Duplicated...................................53

Chapter 13:
Social Media Comparison Is the Devil Wearing Gasoline
Underwear!...56

Chapter 14:
Perception Vs. Reality..59

Chapter 15:
What You See Is What You Get..61

Chapter 16:
Let It Go, Let It Gooo (Sing It with Me!)...........................64

Chapter 17:
There's A Reason the Rearview Mirror Is So Much Smaller Than
the Front Windshield..67

Chapter 18:
Oops I spilled the milk on my carpet, let it sit and spoil or clean it
up..71

Chapter 19:
Damaged Goods, Or Can We Rebrand Ourselves?..........73

Chapter 20:
Shoulda, Coulda, Woulda..84

Chapter 21:
Ignorance Isn't Bliss...87

Chapter 22:
Unnnnhh, No Limits Baby..90

Chapter 23:
Like Nike, Just Do It!..94

Chapter 24:
Speak, Know, Do..97

Chapter 25:
Poison, Poison (Queue BelBivDevoe)................................99

Chapter26:
GASLIGHTING Without the Match 103

Chapter 27:
Meeting People Where They Are....................................109

Chapter 28:
Why Are You Asking Why?..113

Chapter 29:
Don't Take It Personal...117

Chapter 30:
Friends: How Many of Us Have Them?..........................120

Chapter 31:
"Mind Your Business, See" (Will Smith voice)..................124

Chapter 32:
Focus on Your Coin, Honey!..129

Chapter 33:
Student Loans Affect My Ability to Be Bad and Boujee.................132

Chapter 34:
Is My Clock Broken, Or Do I Need Some New Batteries?..........137

Chapter 35:
Single as A Dollar Bill: Does Singleness=Mental Illness?..........139

Chapter 36:
Waiting to Get Picked Up at The Grocery Store....................143

Chapter 37:
Keep It Simple..149

Chapter 38:
To-Go Plate: Last Minute Take-aways...............................152

Chapter 1

Your Boundaries Should be Higher Than Trump's Ego!

Superwoman Karla is always available for other people no matter what. She is the "dependable friend." But lately, Karla has been getting anxiety when people call who typically only do so because they want something. Sound familiar?

Don't explain why you do or don't do something. If you are uncomfortable, end of story-that's reason enough. Stop trying to justify to yourself and others why you have boundaries and why people should respect them. You have them to protect your emotional well-being. It's not your job to educate someone on why you deserve respect. If they care, it's a given. *It's also not your job to set yourself on fire to make sure someone else is warm!* Did you hear me in the back cause I meant that with every fiber of my being? You do not owe anyone but yourself an explanation as to why you move and feel the way you do. Now, this is an easier concept to say than do, but it's a must for a peaceful life.

I don't know why, but I get super uncomfortable exerting my boundaries with anyone. It seriously, really, truthfully makes my butt itch! You're probably laughing, but I'm serious. I fidget a bit just thinking about it. I don't know why this concept is so difficult for me. However, there's no avoiding it. I must draw a line in the sand and make clear what I need. Otherwise, I suffer tremendously later by doing something I know will be detrimental to my physical and mental health. Sometimes, conflict resolution-not confrontation-is necessary to get a clear understanding of what you need. Like all southern aunties have probably said a time or two: a closed mouth doesn't get fed. So, if you aren't telling people what you need, they won't read your mind and figure it out. Nor will they know what your limit is and magically say, "Oops, I think she's had enough!" Let's hold back this time. As much as we may wish people would do right, sometimes they just don't unless we make it understood we're not going!

I also had a problem with getting really upset when people didn't bend over backward for me the way I did for them. I would say: "I can't believe they don't care about me," "I can't believe they wouldn't do this for me," and "I've done a thousand things for them, and they can't just do this one little thing!" Well, it's not that they don't care about you-they just care about themselves more, and they are stating their boundaries of what they want and need no matter how absurd it is. So, instead of getting mad at them for saying what they are going to do, maybe I need to pull back the amount of help I'm giving and/or make sure this person is worthy of that much of my energy. Now I'm not saying I'm not going to help them at all, I'm just putting some limitations on the help I'm going to provide to save myself some frustration in the long run.

A key thing I had to learn the hard way was to never feel guilty for realizing my worth and walking away. No partnership, relationship, friendship, business, etc. is worth sacrificing your self-love and compromising your boundaries for the sake of keeping the peace. **You must go to war on anyone messing with your mental stability.**

When you don't have any boundaries, people get so comfortable asking you the most ridiculous things. I don't know about you, but I find myself getting really frustrated when this happens: *Why would he/she even fix her mouth to ask me that? It's outlandish!* But I must look at myself and realize I created that space where he/she felt comfortable to ask-and also have the idea in his/her head that there is a possibility I will do it. Also, I must not take it personally when people say or do silly things, because it has nothing to do with me as an individual. People are going to ask whoever they think is going to say 'yes.' It could be me, it could be Susie, it could be Johnny-doesn't matter. Their asking has nothing to do with how much they do or don't respect me, or with whether they feel like I do or don't deserve something. It does have everything to do with them testing the water to see whether something's going to bite. So, remind yourself it's okay for them to ask, but it's also okay for you to say no!

To safeguard yourself, give yourself full permission to tell yourself: *It's ok to be alone; it's ok to take some time off; it's ok to speak up; it's ok to not answer a call or text; it's ok to change your mind; it's ok to let go; it's ok to cancel an engagement/commitment, it's ok to do nothing; it's ok to sleep in; it's ok to move on; it's ok to change.* No warning has to be given if this is what's necessary to make sure you don't lose yourself. And please don't let anyone tell you differently. If they do, maybe they don't mean you well. Just a thought.

Superhero evaluation questions to ask yourself:

- Do you feel like your boundaries are appropriate?

- Do you feel uncomfortable with things people ask you to do?

- Are there any people you need to reevaluate your boundaries with?

- Is there a way to place limits on the amount of help you provide so you won't be negatively impacted?

Chapter 2

Is Your Oxygen Mask Secure Before You Help Put on Your Neighbor's?

Superwoman Ariana is very considerate. Her friends and family describe her as nice and loving. She is the "I'll give you the shirt off my back" type of girl. But lately, she's been feeling stressed and finding her daily activities harder to do, and she is unsure why.

When you spend so such time helping other people, it's hard for them to know when *you* need help. How do you use your emergency signal flare? *You can't pour from an empty cup.* I know we've all heard this saying a time or two, but do we ever dive deep into what this means? We are so quick to make sure the people in our lives are encouraged when they are down or having a moment, make sure they have the best birthday parties, attend all their kids' soccer games, etc. Do you find yourself wiping your friends' tears when their companion starts their seasonal "act a fool" syndrome? Are you three or more of your friends' children's godparent? Do you find yourself pulling an Iylana Vanzant calling your friend's significant other to help encourage him/her to get it together? Have you lost count of how much money you've loaned out because you are a personal banker in your spare time? Do you play airport shuttle for your friends instead of letting them take an Uber? Are you an on-call babysitter? Do you find yourself letting family catch a couch for an extended period? Do you downright help protect your people at all costs? Are you the dependable ride or die friend/family member for everyone?

If you are nodding your head to many of these questions, you, my dear, could be that strong friend that may need to be checked on. (And if you said, "Nuh unh, Ashley, I know my limits. I am not doing half of that because I can't overextend myself," ask yourself: Do I have a friend that comes to mind who does fit this mold? If you are the person overusing your friends or family, maybe it's time to give a little more rather than asking so much and check in on your people to make sure they are straight. But back to the strong friend-). If this is you, I need you to speak up, honey! If you're always helping someone else and you never let them know you need help because you don't want to be a "burden", they're going to think you have yourself covered and you're good at handling any and everything. Don't put out false information. You need to give them context and "Blue's Clues" or else they're going to assume you're a superhero without a cape.

People not being there for you or failing to see you need help may leave you frustrated and wondering whether they care. It's not that they don't care, it's simply they don't have a good gauge on when they need to step in and offer support because you are so good at being the helper that they can't see you in the light of being a person who needs to receive help. Going out of your way and helping other people can bring you a lot of joy, but we can unfortunately at times get caught up in the helper role and confused about why we aren't satisfied with ourselves. We are great at noticing others, but horrible at noticing ourselves. We pay more attention and are more concerned about too many other people rather than asking ourselves, "Am I alright?" So, maybe do a weekly or monthly wellness check on yourself to see how you're doing, what you're feeling, and what do you need to feel alright. If you discover you aren't ask yourself what does "feeling good enough" look like to you? When is it time to ask for help? What does help look like to you? Don't dismiss it and convince yourself you're good because you are strong and independent and can deal with anything. Well, yes you can, but why would you want to? And nope, don't use the "I feel weak if I let people know I need help card" because there is strength in recognizing areas that need improvement. You must know when to rest, sis. We aren't race horses. We need to rest and recharge no matter how much we tell ourselves how strong we are. So, take it when you need it. (And don't forget to check on your strong friend!)

Superhero evaluation questions to ask yourself:

- Do you feel like you get enough rest?

- What does rest look like to you?

- Have you ever told the people in your life you are unavailable/no without feeling guilty and/or altering your plans to help them?

- What is your definition of self-care and how often do you practice it? Is this sufficient time for you to practice self-care and if not are you willing to modify the amount of time spent loving on yourself?

- Do you know how to ask for and accept help? If not are you open to learning?

- How do you clue the people in your life in that you need support? Is it clear or muddy waters?

Chapter 3

Is Your Happy Meter Broken?

Superwoman Mya has a "good job," good physical health, is financially stable, and has a great support system. However, she still doesn't feel as though it's enough. She is ashamed to say she is not content as she doesn't want to appear ungrateful, but in reality, she isn't happy.

Have you ever wondered why you can't seem to find the mystical concept called happiness? You wonder does it really exist because it just doesn't seem to apply to you. You ever think is there something wrong with you because this happiness thing is just not happening? Well let me ask you this question what is your definition of happiness because it has different meanings for different people? It's such a personal experience that even though you may ask ten people in your life what happiness means for them that may not be your definition of it. Write down what happiness looks and feels like to you and how would you know if you are there. The reason why I say that is because we must have a measuring scale.

As with most things we do, there must be a metric. Now this can be modified. I just want you to have a more specific concept of what is relevant to you. Another question is are your expectations realistic? Sometimes and I'm not saying that's the case here, we have expectations that are a bit much and hard to obtain. Example we will not consider ourselves happy until we've won the lotto and all our money troubles are gone but you don't play the lotto (tilts head in confusion). Maybe give yourself some short term and long-term goals you'd like to see happen for yourself that are not so overwhelming to work on. Also consider not having any expectations at all on certain things. I know for me I am a very goal-oriented person, so when I set out to do something, I always have a goal I like to reach for. The problem with that is when I don't reach the goal, I'm no longer having fun. I no longer feel happy and all I'm thinking about is how can I make sure I reach that goal. Knowing this about myself, I had to separate certain activities to say if it's for leisure or for business. If it's for leisure, then there's no expectation. I'm just going to have fun, see how it goes and keep an open mind. Now if it's career-related then yes, I'm going to think about goals and things I can do to be successful. Maybe ask yourself whether you have expectations for a lot of areas in your life. Do you expect your happiness to be attributed to others? Because if we depend on others for our happiness, we are in for a roller coaster ride of disappointment.

People are so fickle they change their mind all the time it's like a role of the dice. If we're relying on other people to dictate our happiness we are not going to get a stable answer. It's going to vary from person to person personality to personality. So, maybe consider using yourself as the only gauger so as not to be frustrated when you get different responses from different people. People can make you smile, blush, stroke your ego or illicit various emotion's in you but they cannot be responsible for your overall happiness. That's not to say they can never make you joyful. For example if you see them and you're excited because you enjoy spending time with that person this is plausible. But your overall mental stability they can't be in control of. Again, happiness is a single person sport. No team players. Only you are responsible for your happiness as well as your healing that I discussed in other parts of the book. Ask yourself how often you guard your mind from getting undesirable information from what you see and hear, which becomes your thoughts and our feelings. And thoughts determine, how we perceive life. Since we are not happy, the driving feeling to achieve our ultimate goal in life is: unlimited happiness. Also, remember even the happiest person is not happy a hundred percent of the time 24/7, 365 days. They're human just like you so they experience other emotions such as anger, sadness, fear, loneliness etc. So, even though you see them and they appear to be happy, just know not a single person walking this Earth is always happy all day every day. I encourage you to do a journal every day asking yourself one thing you're thankful for, one thing you enjoyed about the day, one thing you learned from the day, one person you enjoyed speaking to and what your goal is for the next day. Possibly do this in the morning so that way you have a framework for your day and maybe evaluate at the end of the day how you did and what you can do differently if you didn't like the day. Possibly take the social aspect from happiness because sometimes we gauge our happy meter based off what we see on social media or in society and we think that's what we're supposed to feel, think and do in order to be happy.

So, again make it a personal journey-like writing in your diary. This is not something you would share with the world, not something you would compare with the world. It's a personal thing you keep for yourself. Your happiness is the same concept and FYI negative thoughts and emotions often follow negative behaviors which, not by coincidence, follows negative experiences. It becomes an endless cycle that often results in more and more unhappiness. Negative thoughts often come from low self-esteem, chemical imbalances, unpleasant past experiences, and so on. Possibly do a depression screening with a mental health professional. If you don't feel comfortable doing that look for one online and see if you have any symptoms of depression because sometimes you can do all the things I mentioned and it still not bring about any results. It's a possibility there may be clinical depression going on which in that case I would say consult with your local health care provider so that way you guys can come up with a plan on how to address this so you can live the life you desire because it is possible.

Superhero evaluation questions to ask yourself:

- What do you feel would make you happy? Is this tangible/realistically obtainable?

- Do you feel you are doing all you can do to obtain the happiness you seek? If not, what actions are you consistently committed to doing and how will this be measured?

- What does happiness look like to you? Do you think it's a realistic picture?

- Are you taking the steps necessary to obtain your definition of Happiness?

- Are you comparing your happiness to other people's versions of happiness?

- Does your happiness involve other people-and if so, do you think this is healthy?

Chapter 4

How Many Dependents Are You Claiming on Those Taxes?

Superwoman Skylar feels down that her boss has not recognized and complimented her for the hard work she displayed on a big project. Add this to the fact that she recently had a dramatic cut/style change with her hair that she loved, but her boyfriend wasn't feeling it, so now she thinks it was a mistake. Does this resonate with you?

    I think one of the hardest lessons I've had to learn in the past year is not depending on other people to make me happy. I know that sounds cliché and I see all these great sayings about how your happiness comes from within and all this other blah blah blah but there's so much truth to that. I have this bad habit of reaching out to other people when I'm making a big decision. I know what I want to do and how I want to handle it. I often just need someone else to confirm with me that it's okay for me to take that step. Crazy right? They're not doing anything but saying yes or no so I'm ok with moving forward. I've asked myself repeatedly why I need somebody else to tell me what I have already thought of, planned and how I should feel about something that I know is going to significantly impact my life. Why am I involving so many people to get that confirmation? To be honest it's because I don't trust myself. I don't feel like I'm enough. I had to rely on other people for validation and that's a dangerous thing to do because who better to tell me about me than me? It made me think about other areas in my life that I'm depending on other people and it was kind of scary to realize I have a lot of dependent personality traits. Now I know what you're thinking, and no, I don't have dependent personality disorder, but I did realize my happiness was based off of other people's happiness. For example, I like doing things for other people. I like putting smiles on their faces. I like helping people, and I realize that made me feel good about myself. However I don't do that for myself on the regular basis. I don't put myself in that equation and say, "Hey, what do *I* like? What do *I* want that helps *me* get through the day?" That's because I didn't deem it as important, but what's odd is that I think other people's happiness is important. There has been past relationships where how that person feels about me or how they treated me dictated how I viewed myself. But the reality is I'm a badass whether I'm with this guy or I'm not this person's friend. So, why am I basing my self-perception on how I'm valued by other people? The reality of it is I have no dependents. I'm head of household so I can act as such, which means I can stop trying to base how I feel about myself on how other people feel about me or think I am supposed to act and be and really ask myself who do I want to be, what do I want to stand for, and also really come to terms with how I feel about myself. Now this can be a painful thing if you find out how low your perception is of yourself, but there's beauty in building a new outlook.

My grandmother-God rest her soul-was three months shy of 90 years old when she died. Only had a junior high education level, was born in 1925, and had 14 kids, so school was not a priority for her. My mother and her siblings all were hard workers many of them working 20, 30, and sometimes 40 years at a company because they wanted a "good job." A few of them were able to obtain trades and later in life after their children were out of the house degrees. However school was not as big of a priority for them as well because they were focused on working and not living in poverty like my grandmother. Then comes my generation. College was heavily pushed as they wanted me and many of my other female cousins to get an education, not have to rely on a man nor have children at an early age. I think their intentions were good and they meant well. However they spent so much attention on making us the strong independent black women who had a "good job" if you had money in the bank and didn't have to work long hours. But they really didn't spend a whole lot of time teaching us about the importance of self-care and being mentally at peace as well as how to be good wives/mothers. Now don't get me wrong I think they are phenomenal mothers who gave the best they could with what they had. But with that being said I think many people in my generation lost this, somewhere in the message that having a man and needing a man was not a bad thing. I think they thought they had to be this strong independent black woman hear me roar, I can do it all by myself and put it as a weakness to have a man. But if you look back at all your aunties and your Big Mama's they were doing it with their husbands. Your grandma made it work with your papa. No I'm not saying drop out of your graduate program and stop working like it's 1950. I'm just saying there's nothing negative or wrong with a woman admitting hey I need a man for companionship or hey I want a man in my life to help me with my children That is not a sign of weakness ladies. And if we want to go biblical, they said two are better than one. Now let me not discriminate because it's 2019 so sis if you said hey, I need or want a woman nothing wrong with that either. Point is we have to stop making it seem like it's a weakness because we desire companionship, love and support. That's what we are put on Earth to do which is love: give it and receive it. Personally, I can't wait until my husband finds me so he can take this trash out and mow this yard because I'm sick of it, you hear me sick of it all! I don't want to touch the trash can ever again in my life once I get married, ha-ha!

Now this brings me to my next chapter: marriage plus babies do not equal happiness. I know I went through a period of my life where I watched a lot of my friends and family who are in my age bracket get married, have one, two, three babies, get divorced and remarried again. I felt like something in my life was missing like I wasn't whole because I'm not in that phase of my life yet. I'm excited to get to that phase of my life. But my life is pretty awesome right now. I had a hard time seeing that, so I made myself write down all the things I want to accomplish before I become a wife and a mother. I was surprised at how many things I want to do, and I didn't realize I had so many things that I still want to accomplish before I enter a new phase. So, instead of me focusing on how depressed I am that I'm not in the same phase of life as other people. I've started the journey of doing those things that I still want to do, and it's been fun. For example there are countries I want to go to that I know wouldn't be feasible if I had a husband and child such as Egypt. There's no way I would feel comfortable leaving my husband and child for two weeks with limited cell phone to visit Cairo. But I can do that now while I'm single. I joked with myself that I could be majorly depressed at home or a little depressed seeing the world. I chose the latter.

Also I'm branching out and starting my own business full time. I would be terrified to take a risk of quitting my Corporate America job with health benefits with a family. However, since it's just me I can take the risks and make the mistakes without it negatively affecting anyone else. I'm also writing the book you're reading right now. I don't know if I would have had time to write this book or would have even convinced myself to have the confidence enough to write before. But now it's on my bucket list and you're reading it so that means I have accomplished yet another thing on my list. Point is I don't want you thinking that you're not going to be whole until you experience being someone's misses or mommy. Those are beautiful blessings and personally I can't wait to experience them but I'm also going to have a hell of a life and not hold my breath until that happens for me. Don't get me wrong it's not always sunshine and roses and sometimes it does get difficult to see other people receiving those blessings that your heart so strongly desires. I encourage you during those difficult times to go back to your list and think of the things you want to do that can increase your happiness. Also your feelings are valid so if you're having these thoughts and feelings don't diminish, downplay or keep it to yourself. Have that conversation with somebody else who is going to be able to lift you up when you're having a down moment.

Superhero evaluation questions to ask yourself:

- Are you in the "here and now" of your life, or focused on the past/future?

- Do you feel as though you have an accurate picture of other people's lifestyle you want, or are you only viewing the "pros."

Chapter 5

Me Time: I'm Lonely, But Shhh, Don't Tell Anyone

Superwoman Tamara is a 31-year-old single female. She is not involved in any romantic relationships, has moved to a city ten hours away from her hometown, and has not established meaningful friendships in her new city.

First it's ok to admit what you are feeling. We often are ashamed of this word but it's a feeling we all have felt at one time or another. The sooner we acknowledge it the sooner we can remedy it. I spent a few months of 2017 severely struggling with loneliness in silence. When I finally mustered up enough courage to tell my friends/family they were shocked. None of them had a clue that I was struggling with this as I felt I had a million people around me, but no one who actually saw me.

Loneliness is like hunger. When your stomach is growling and you haven't eaten, you don't get mad at your body for being hungry- you find something to eat. In that same token if you are lonely don't get mad, feel ashamed, afraid to speak up, or stay in that lonely feeling. Figure out ways to offset your loneliness or what if anything is causing your loneliness. Most commonly being around other people helps. For example: if you are single and desire companionship but for whatever reason it hasn't happened for you, yet while I agree it sucks your husband Idris didn't come home last night, ask yourself what realistic action you can take in the meantime until he gets off work. Here are a few suggestions although you are not limited to these that may help with loneliness:

1. Reach out to a friend you haven't spoken to in a while. They may appreciate you checking in with them.

2. If you have grandparents or elderly relatives spend some time with them. We often think/feel as though we have unlimited opportunities to reach out to them, but truth is you don't, so cherish soaking up their knowledge, learning your family history, getting that good ole fashioned cooking, hugs because they give the best ones etc. .

3. Can you volunteer or get involved with a nonprofit you are passionate about. For example: big brother big sister, fight against hunger, afterschool tutoring, etc. . These organizations always need extra support as they are often short staffed and you can serve your community while being around others.

4. Join your cities sport league or create a team for flag football, softball, volleyball, kickball, etc.

5. If you are in a sorority/fraternity become active if you aren't.

6. Maybe group comradery would be nice. Meetup is a great site for local events.

7. Weekly lunch with friends, family, coworkers. Create an ongoing event. It gives you something to look forward to. Try new spots or themes of food or possibly cook and invite people over.

8. Weekend brunch/try a new spot once a month and send out a fb event to see who is interested

9. Take dance lessons. Whether it's swing out, salsa, line dance, or hip hop. Most dance classes require a partner which means you have to be around people and actively engaged. It's hard to stay lonely when those feet are foot loose and fancy free.

10. Join a book club or read a book. I'm sure if you don't have a Kindle/iPad there is a library within a one to mile radius from you and those books are free. If time/your schedule is an issue, look into virtual book clubs.

11. Babysit for friends/family. They'll think you are a God send and kids love one on one attention and adventures. I took my niece to a science museum one time when I was lonely. We stayed four hours, had a ball and my brother was happy to enjoy a Sunday sports day kid free.

12. Learn a foreign language. I know in my area meetup has free groups for conversational fun. I was able to brush up on my Spanish.

13. Binge watch a tv show someone has been telling you about, hit up that good girlfriend of yours and see if she wants to order snacks/drinks so you guys can Netflix and chill while catching up. People are so busy these days sometimes it's hard to really find time. This would be a perfect time to see if you missed some things going on in their world while you

guys are pigginig out and laughing. Nothing like a good old-fashioned sleep over.

14. Do speaking engagements if you feel bold in areas that you consider yourself a subject matter expert.

15. Pamper yourself-go to the spa for a facial, mani/pedi, massage, or a little retail therapy within your budget.

16. Don't just join a church join the ministry to be involved and connected to the members and the community.

17. Group fitness such as cross fit, run club, pole fitness, Zumba. It's nice not to be the only one huffing and puffing.

18. Road trip to visit that family, friend, or soror you're always promising you'll get together with but your schedules never align to realistically see them.

You are not limited to this list. I just want to get your mind thinking of ways to cope with loneliness. Whatever you choose is up to you. I just want you to act immediately. Don't wait and tell yourself I'll do such and such the first of the week to have a fresh start or that you can wait until next month or after you finish a project at work, or a season ends when you have "more time." There's never a perfect time in our busy schedules. We must consciously make time. Be proactive in managing your loneliness before it manages you.

Superhero evaluation questions to ask yourself:

- Are you aware of when you are feeling lonely?

- Do you feel embarrassed to let other people know you suffer from loneliness? If so why is their shame in your honesty?

- What do you do to combat your loneliness?

- Do you find it helpful or do you feel you need to reevaluate things to help when you experience this emotion?

Chapter 6

Feelings, All in My Feelings

Superwoman Jaci has difficulty expressing herself as she does not want to appear weak. She is sometimes passive-aggressive in her communication and waits until someone makes her super angry before lashing out on this person.

No one gets permission to tell you how you should feel, for how long, or if it's right or wrong. It's not what you feel but what you do with the feelings once you process what emotion you are experiencing. Some people are very emotional. Nothing wrong with that-it's just a part of their personality. But our society has placed such a negative stigma on people transparently expressing their emotions that we sometimes don't express them. We've been conditioned into the awful habit of masking how we truly feel or forcing ourselves to feel differently for fear of being perceived as weak or dramatic. We shy away from vulnerability.

We as women have to constantly remind ourselves that we are human and it's okay to feel good or bad. The important thing is what you do with the feelings once you feel them. We all wish we could feel the good vibe only energy all the time but it's not reality. When something frustrates or upset us, we want to feel better as soon as possible. We don't want to wait. We want an immediate result to stop feeling bad. So, sometimes we convince ourselves we're okay when maybe we're not fine. We put on this fake plastic smile, say we are good, or enjoy cutting the person off that caused us to feeling anything, say how much better we are now that a certain thing is over. But then we pull off like Red from Friday, go in the car and cry as if someone stole our chain. After we shed that last thug tear we tell ourselves how pathetic and irrational we are since we are actually expressing our current mood. Now seriously what sense does that make that you are punishing yourself for being human? Rather people express it or not everyone feels emotions. That's why you have those famous feelings charts in most doctor offices and why if I said a word such a sad happy, afraid, worried, scared you'd know exactly what I'm talking about. Because you've experienced it multiple times in your life as has every human being walking on this Earth has. Now FYI you only get roughly three Kanye moments a year. The rest of the time I need you working on processing those 1000 feelings going through that pretty little head of yours. So, this is what I need you to do moving forward after you read this chapter. One I need you to honestly state how you feel. Move past the facade that is your knee-jerk reaction of saying you are fine and give a label to what your actual emotion is.

Admit it to yourself. You owe yourself honesty. Two find the source what led you to feel this emotion. Was it something that was said that offended you? Did an event or something specific trigger this? I need you to find out where it came from. Three stay woke! It's okay to have your moment and if that requires vulnerability find a safe space to really address your true sentiment. Don't tell yourself you're doing too much or that you are being irrational. Maybe you are not doing enough and the only thing that's irrational is dealing with your feelings in an unhealthy way but not the feeling itself. If it's conflict resolution with somebody else be respectful yet honest and let's not dance around the issue. Put it out there with hopes of a solution. Know your feelings are your property and it's okay to let yourself feel them. They don't belong to anybody else so that means no one else has a say so on how you feel and how you deal because their name is not on the deed. Four run it: I need you to let the emotion play all the way out. Don't diminish it or cut it off before it's done. Take the time you need to heal and know that feelings are fickle meaning, they can change at the drop of a dime. For example have you ever been in a good mood like maybe your flat twist came out popping and then you walk outside, it's raining, and you forgot your umbrella and now your hair is ruined. So, now you're frustrated but then a cute person walks by, lets you share their umbrella and compliments you so now you're blushing and feeling good about yourself again. Often in a two-minute time frame we can go through many emotions, sometimes hundreds of emotions within a day. So, know that no feeling is final. It's a moment and moments are temporary and will pass.

Do you have those days where you just want to give a big ugly whine but don't because it'll make you look like a punk because you're crying since life is just kicking your tail? Sometimes you have to let it out, sometimes you have to roll with that big tantrum just to get it out of your system. There's nothing wrong with having a bad day because a bad day doesn't mean a bad life. Sometimes it just means you're just having one of those days when you've done enough todaying for today. Why are we holding it in? Release. Let it happen. It doesn't mean you have to cry the whole day, but there's nothing wrong with just having 10 or 15 minutes to say this s*%@ is real and hard! There's no instructional manual to life. If there was, I'd be picking up the first copy. With that being said sometimes we just don't know what to say, what to do, how to move forward or where to go from where we currently are, sometimes it gets stressful and sometimes because you don't know what to do or how to move you'll get overwhelmed. When this happens a good cry just may be in order before a solution can be created.

Superhero evaluation questions to ask yourself:

- Are you comfortable with experiencing varied emotions?

- How do you express them?

- Do emotions equate to weakness and/or vulnerability for you?

- Do you feel you have healthy coping mechanisms and/or stress relievers? If so, what are they? If not, are there any new mechanisms you'd be willing to try?

Chapter 7

Your Healing Is Your Responsibility

Superwoman Nicole had a very traumatic childhood as well as a strained relationship with her parents due to her upbringing. She holds resentment for her parents as she felt they have negatively affected her adulthood. Her parents do not seem remorseful for their drug use and her unstable childhood which prevents her from forgiving her parents as she feels she's entitled to an apology.

It's not on you that maybe your mom didn't win mother of the year and damaged your self-esteem or Day Day your ex-boyfriend cheated, someone stole from you, etc. . That's not your fault that bad things were said/done to you, but it is on you to heal expeditiously. It can be someone's fault that you were hurt, broke, affected etc. . But it's *solely* your responsibility to fix it not theirs. And yes that's a hard pill to swallow because maybe you didn't ask for or deserve what happened/what was said to you and they haven't corrected their course of action. But it is still your responsibility to determine how you are going to deal with past traumas and make a life out of it, how to take that pain, how to overcome and build a happy life for yourself post experience(s). Fault and responsibility ultimately don't go together. The person who wronged you is not responsible for corrective action especially when it's affecting your heart, your life, your happiness. Your happiness and peace of mind is your responsibility only. Everyone walking this earth is only obligated to themselves. We choose to be considerate of other people, but we are only indebted to heal ourselves. We can go all day about who wronged us and who's at fault and more than likely there is merit to your claim. But that finger pointing keeps you paralyzed in victim or what I like to also call wounded person mode. Have you ever seen a wounded dog that you are trying to help, but the dog almost bites your hand off if you get close to him/her. You know you come in peace, but the dog is hurt and doesn't know what to do so they attack to protect themselves. When you're in this mode you are stuck in suffering. How you heal is taking ultimate responsibility and figuring out how to make it happen so you are at peace with yourself regardless of who's to blame. We want to switch you from victim to survivor mode. Now this can be tough because sometimes you were innocent and something bad just happened to you whom I can assume is a good person and possibly the person who did/said that bad thing(s) did not receive the karma you felt he/she deserved. Although it royally sucks for me to put this out there and please don't shoot the messenger, it's unfortunately none of your business their karma. As much as the mischievous person in us wants to see some vindication, the ultimate good human being in us isn't with revenge and we must let them deal with their own emotional baggage surrounding their life choices. Taking responsibility is a recognition of the power you obtain when you stop blaming people- it's not letting them off the hook or saying it is ok to treat you any old kind of way-you are now activating your emotional self-defense and no longer being powerless. It's you taking your power back.

Reminder: You are responsible for your own happiness. You are responsible for your own healing. It is your job to forgive people even if they are not sorry (forgiving doesn't mean allowing unhealthy back people in your space). It is your job to figure out what peace looks like to you. It is your job to work on building your self-esteem and to be very mindful of limiting your access to people who threaten what you work to build on. It is your job to rid yourself of people who don't have your best interest at heart and once you realize that not give them repeated opportunities to hurt you in any shape form or fashion.

Superhero evaluation questions to ask yourself:

- What would you do if you never got the apology you feel you deserve?

- How would you move past such painful memories?

- Do you feel you're making any progress in your healing?

- Is there a support group such as friends, family, a religious organization, or counseling that you can attend to help aid your healing?

Chapter 8

I Thought Therapy Was for Crazy People (which I'm not)!

Superwoman Krista was raised in a Southern Baptist church. Her parents are heavily involved in the ministry. Typically, when Krista has a problem, her parents' first response is, "Pray about it." Krista has been feeling overwhelmed with her life and has considered counseling. However, her parents have discouraged this and told her she needs to be more involved in the church as she has shied away from it after graduating college.

I'm not sure where in our society we deemed needing professional mental health as a bad thing and maybe I'm a little biased because I am in the field, but we must stop this untruth immediately. Like don't pass go, don't collect $200, act immediately. There are too many people suffering in silence, and I don't want you to be one of them. Have you noticed how many celebrities are committing suicide or even people in your everyday life? You and others are shocked that a person was at that state in life. It's because they did not feel comfortable enough to proactively receive the help and once it became so severe it was difficult to manage. I need you to really marinate on this, if your primary care physician informed you that you were diabetic and needed to take insulin would you question it? If you had a rash for three weeks and it progressively worsened would you not schedule an apt to see a dermatologist? If you did and he/she prescribed you a cream to treat a possible skin infection would you second guess your need for the cream, not go to your local pharmacy to fill the prescription and pray the rash goes away? Sounds silly right? If you know you need medical treatment you go without hesitation, pay that copay and get what you need asap to remedy that ailment. So, why is it so different for mental health? Why do we automatically go to the extreme and think because we need a trained medical professional to help us deal with mental health that it equates to us being emotionally unstable, hesitate to call such medical professional, become embarrassed that we may benefit from the assistance, ashamed and secretive to inform family/friends we attend if we are brave enough to make the call? What is the worst that could happen if you pray *and* get help at the same time? Why do we have to do one or the other? What if the Lord gave you the resources of health insurance, a car to drive to the appointment, and an available counselor who you vibe with to help you through whatever life has thrown your way?

Superhero evaluation questions to ask yourself:

- Would you ever consider counseling? Why or why not?

- What are your expectations from counseling? What are your thoughts about going?

- Do you have health insurance that can cover this, or does your employer have an employee assistance program that can help you pay for the first few sessions?

- What type of counselor are you looking for?

- What type of hours do you have available to see a counselor?

- How many times per month can you go?

- Do you have any friends or family that have ever been to counseling? Would you consider asking about their experiences?

- (For those who are very spiritual or religious) Do you feel that you can simultaneously go to counseling and church?

- Do you feel that your spiritual advisor is qualified to help with your mental health?

Chapter 9

Do Not Disturb-Block Is Your Best Friend

Superwoman Bailey is not familiar with the 'Do Not Disturb' button on her phone. A friend suggested she try it and take a break from her ever-demanding schedule. However, she was hesitant to do so as she'd like to be available just in case family or friends-or even her job-needs her. She is afraid that important deadlines will be missed if she takes a break. She feels as though there's always something that needs to be done or she could be working on.

Sometimes you have to have some "me time" to regroup. Self-care is so important and necessary to keep us mentally healthy. Sometimes we feel uncomfortable hoarding time for ourselves as we think about items we can be checking off our to do lists or the time we could be spending with the spouse, kids, family, friends, etc. But think about it this way: if you kept a light on in a specific room in your house 24 hours a day, 7 days a week, what would happen? It would eventually burn out. However, if you turn the light off when you're not in the room and don't need to use the electricity, guess what? You preserve energy and that light bulb lasts a lot longer. Your body and mental health are no different. Sometimes, you have to turn the light off. I'm pretty sure your typical day is so jam-packed that sometimes you don't even have a moment to think about what's good or not good for yourself. Well, when you put yourself on 'do not disturb,' you can have those moments. Occasionally, you have to say 'no' to that invite to a social gathering, sometimes, you have to tell your family and friends 'no' you can't help them with their situation, and sometimes it's okay to not answer the phone every blue moon. Put yourself on 'do not disturb' so no one can have access to you until you're ready for them. Turn your phone off! You are not obligated to answer no matter how many times they call or text! You don't have to explain why you didn't answer a phone you pay the bill for, nor do you have to justify how often you recharge to keep yourself from pulling a Brittney Spears circa 2007 "shaving head" moment. Do what you have to do, hon. Do not feel ashamed because you are not locked and loaded 24/7. It's just not a realistic characteristic of being human. And no, it's not selfish! It's called self-care! Selfishness is (of a person, action, or motive) lacking consideration for others; concerned chiefly with one's own personal profit or pleasure. Self-care is the practice of taking action to preserve or improve one's own health. Big difference right?!

Superhero evaluation questions to ask yourself:

- Do you know how to rest and relax? How often do you do this?

- What does rest and relaxation look like to you?

- Do you ever take mental health days for yourself without feeling guilty?

- How do you implement that into your busy schedule? Does your good have merit?

Chapter 10

Limit Your "Clap Backs," Sis

Superwoman Sean has been classified by her friends as the "queen of clapback." If someone comes for her and they weren't sent, she politely lets them know where they can go. She has no issues getting people together and "reading them" for filth.

I am a survivor of child abuse. I often feel like I didn't have a voice and I was scared out of my mind to ever speak up when I was wronged because of the abuse that would follow. So, when I finally did find that voice I went through a phase where I was always letting people know they couldn't treat me any kind of way, they couldn't say certain things and it was very specific things you couldn't do to me. I was Ashley and you was gone get this work if you came at me wrong. It was to the point where I feel like it was overkill. Meaning sometimes the clap back they deserved was on a level two but I hit them with a level seven clap back because I had to let the message come across loud and clear I'm not the one boo boo!! I developed this reputation of being overly aggressive in my communication and I didn't like that because I felt like well, they came for me and I didn't send for them so I can let them know so they wouldn't come for me again. But I realized that all people saw was an aggressive female. They didn't see what the person did to offend me only my response and I didn't like that perception. I also didn't like all the energy it took for me to clap back every time someone offended me. Now let me be crystal clear. I'm not saying be anybody's walking doormat, but I am saying ask yourself does the infraction deserve your attention. When I was honest with myself some of those offenses didn't deserve a response. They could be ignored. So, I have this little rule that I borrowed from somebody which is to ask myself will this matter to me in five minutes, will it matter to me in five hours, will it matter to me in five days, will it matter to me in five weeks, will it matter to me in five months, will it matter to me in five years? If the answer is no to most of those questions, sis, let it go! I repeat, Let It Go! My grandmother once asked me if a dog is walking down the road and it barks at every tree in its path in a very wooded area how long would it take for that dog to walk a mile: probably forever! Don't let these small annoyances prevent you from reaching your destination.

Superhero evaluation questions to ask yourself:

- Does every confrontation deserve a response from you?

- Do you feel you have the power to restrain yourself with your logic and not give into your feelings when someone comes for you?

- Do you feel like it's a personal attack when people say or do things that are offensive or show a lack of character on their part?

- Do you feel like you expel a lot of energy telling people how it is?

- Is there any validity to what people say about you? Do you feel secure about who you are as a person?

Chapter 11

Viewer's Choice

Superwoman Desiree is a true "keeping up with the Joneses" girl. The opinions of others carry much weight when it comes to how she lives her day-to-day life. She is often worried about not appearing to have it all together as well as keeping up with the good girl image she has maintained since her high school days.

We have a tendency to be so focused on what people are going to say or think that we operate differently than how we would if no one was watching. Why are other people's perceptions so important to us? People will always have an opinion about what you should or shouldn't do or say, and they're entitled to that. However, you're also entitled to not listen or to take what they say with a grain of salt. Also, remember people only like to showcase their winnings and not their losses. People sometimes fabricate events to make themselves seem bigger than they truly are. So, you may be hesitant to move in your real life based on others fictional lifestyle. The goal is to truly be successful, happy, and at peace-not just appear to be winning in these categories from a perception based standpoint. So, if we spend most of our energy trying to paint a certain picture to a made-up audience of naysayers, there will be little to no energy spent on achieving the real goals. What would you do if no one was watching? Would you offer an opinion, or judge how others are living? Or would you live with a little less pressure of your own decisions?

Superhero evaluation questions to ask yourself:

- How would you behave if no one was watching?

- Why is another person's opinion about your life so important to you?

- Are you proud of the woman you've become? If not, why not and what are you presently doing to be proud of yourself?

Chapter 12

The Original Cannot Be Duplicated

Superwoman Felicity is a true trendsetter. She prides herself on having the latest hairstyle and designer purses. She renews the lease on her car every three years to stay current as she wants to be a socialite. If there's an "in crowd," she's not going to sit outside of it.

Why do we spend so much time trying to blend in with the masses? I see so many people with similar fashionnova dresses, weave color like their favorite rapper/singer, driving the same cars, going to the same social outings, doing the same one leg poses for Instagram, houses decorated in similar style etc. . And don't get me wrong I'm not saying there's anything wrong with getting what you like and what you've worked hard to obtain. I'm just saying occasionally I'm curious if you have certain things because you really wanted it that way as an individual or because so many other people have it and you think you need to as well. We've become this herd of cattle to do like so and so did. When I look on social media I see most with the same hairstyle, clothing, and business (women: hair, makeup, clothing line, model, socialite, dudes: fitness, sports, musician with the beard of course). It's like we are all looking at the same clones. When did being original go out of style? Do you know there's no one else as dope as you in the world. I mean literally no one else is exactly like you. To me it's so cool to explore your uniqueness yet we dedicate so much energy trying to fit in. Have you asked yourself what about you as an individual is amazing that the masses isn't doing and what this truly represents?

Believe it or not, most will continue to paint that picture for that audience of whatever number of friends/followers you have on online. Social media is a very cool and interesting tool, but that's not the place to build your confidence or to get confirmation for something regarding your life. So, many issues-or it may not be an issue to you, so let's just say "difficult tasks"-starts at such an early stage you don't recognize it's a part of you who are. You buying something, going somewhere, or joining something is all a part of you trying to get applause from that audience that you think is waiting to offer you approval. Life is better, in my opinion, when you wake up and go about your day not worried about the outcome of anything because you're not looking for approval of any kind.

Superhero evaluation questions to ask yourself:

- What about you makes you stand out from the crowd? Name one unique quality about yourself that you value and you are glad you possess?

- Do you feel comfortable or uncomfortable if you're an anomaly in a situation?

Chapter 13

Social Media Comparison Is the Devil Wearing Gasoline Underwear!

Superwoman Kadesha checks her social media pages in the morning before she even gets out of bed and brushes her teeth. She often looks to her peers to see how her life measures up in comparison. If she finds an area that she feels she is lacking in, she thinks she's not doing enough and has failed in some way.

You're a bold-faced lie (fibber if you had that old school grandma who felt like the word "lie" was a curse word, lol) if you say you've never compared yourself to others on Snapchat, Facebook, Instagram, etc. Did you know there is actually a psychological term for it called social comparison theory. No, seriously, take a look (https://www.psychologytoday.com/basics/social-comparison-theory). But if you are not interested in this tidbit of information, let's carry on…

I know I can't be the only one who does it. You know you're on that Android/iPhone and see your friends/family/colleagues online getting married in Aruba and The Obamas are at the wedding, having a billion and one kids, buying a new house/foreign car, traveling the world, wearing designer clothes, etc. …and while you're genuinely happy for them, you can't help but create that side by side comparison of how awesome are they and how lame I am feeling. Why do we do this to ourselves? How do we know people aren't social media stunting, you know putting on for the gram with knock off clothes, leased cars they are three months behind on the note, staying with their parents, in an unhealthy relationship reenacting a love and hip hop scene, etc. Now I hope none of this is happening to your peeps, because you never wish badly on people. IJS whether they are doing exceptionally well, ok or lying why do we compare their best to our worst? (Raises hand) I know I've been guilty of doing this, I'm a legit frequent comparison member. I'm perfectly fine until I scroll a bit too long and then start to think of where I am in life and where others are and feel I am lacking in x, y and z area. If you're a religious person here's a good verse to help you out of the comparison blues-2 Corinthians 10:12 – For we dare not make ourselves of the number or compare ourselves with some that commend themselves: but they measuring themselves by themselves, and comparing themselves among themselves, are not wise. But if you are heathen and don't care about such scriptures then a better question is…

How do we stop or decrease this bad habit?

1. Do some self-reflection (which isn't a bad thing), as to possible areas in your life that you may be a bit insecure about and maybe assess why is this such a sore spot with you. **Insecurities.** Yeah, I said it. I know we dread this word, but you have it so why not explore it and do something to change this possibly unrealistic thought, fear, doubt, irrational theory etc. …

2. Maybe set a time limit for how long you'll get on social media each day. Maybe a one-five minute limit and click off the app(s). I know it's hard but fight the urge MAN (Martin Voice)!!!

3. Are you realizing the amazing people you have in your life? I mean while we all love being nosy and seeing what's going on with others, why not see what's going on in your "real friends' lives." Maybe call/text a friend or agree to meet and catch up on life, get a good keke, holla at that $5 happy hour, set a play date if you have kids, whatever. Maybe a quick reminder that you have solid people on your team that you may can enjoy more because as the old cliché saying goes "life is short" so you might as well be as happy in it as you can with the meaningful people in your circle.

4. Follow up on you hobbies/things you love. We are all super busy so why not take some time to do what you love. Or if you don't have something you love then why not get creative in testing out things to find a hobby. Create an I'll try it list of restaurants you want to taste, events you'd like to attend, social functions, learn to play an instrument, start learning how to do hair, IDK ladies just try something!!

5. Get to moving. I'm sure we could all be overdue for some exercise to drop that freshman 15 that's still here 10+ years later. Go walking, running, biking, catch that $10 Planet Fitness membership (we all can afford that, but if not, do some at home exercises using YouTube).

Chapter 14

Perception Vs. Reality

Superwoman Yasmine feels as though she's not where she should be at the age of 40. Even though she works for a great company, enjoys her job, has a supportive partner, and enjoys a great support system, she often feels as though she is an imposter and does not deserve her life.

Just because you *feel* a certain way about yourself doesn't mean it's true. Perception doesn't always mean its reality. We oftentimes confuse the two thinking because you think and feel something very strongly then it is an absolute especially if we have a negative view of ourselves. We will believe the negative ten times faster than the positive concerning ourselves. Occasionally we even have the nerve to question if the positive is true and/or we are being too cocky if we compliment ourselves too much and recognize our greatness. Now isn't that something? But that's incorrect thinking. For example, let's say I am sitting in a room with a two month old baby and feel as though this newborn is aggressive, threatening and makes me nervous with his/her scary behavior. Now this is an extreme example and I know you are probably thinking is she stable in the mind because what the heck kind of example is that. But just go with me here for a second. The reality is a newborn is probably sleep or sitting there looking around not doing much of anything, but my feelings seem very real. I feel threatened. But that's not the facts of what's going on. However it is my perception. In this instance my perception is not reality. (Let's define perception as the prescription glasses we use to view ourselves and the world around us we are observing. Reality is the true essence of things or generally stated how things really are no matter if we perceive it to be or not. Reality trumps feelings, expectations, beliefs and thoughts. Our perception can sometimes cloud our reality even when we are unaware.) It is up to us to consciously realize they are not always one in the same. *How do you do that?* You ask. Simple:

Perception does *not* equal *reality*.
Remember-facts over feelings.

Here's an exercise to help:

On a sheet of paper, draw a line in the middle and write 'feelings' on one side, and 'facts' on the other. View this list and counter negative thoughts when you get overwhelmed by looking at the facts. No matter how you feel about the situation the facts don't lie.

Chapter 15

What You See Is What You Get

Superwoman Desna has a hard time seeing herself the way others see her. When she receives compliments, she has a hard time accepting and believing them to be true.

Learn to love all of what's staring back at you when you wake up to look in the mirror and kill the dragon breath. We spend so much time thinking about what we wish was bigger, smaller, and flatter that we often lose sight of our current goodness. For me it was a long excruciating journey to be comfortable physically with myself. Some people have even said flat out to my face chick are you crazy you're beautiful, cute, you're fine, nothing is wrong with you, etc. . But I just didn't see it. I'm pretty sure it attributes to my physical and verbal abuse at a young age. However as I've said somewhere in this book, I had to figure out how to accept myself: the good, the bad and ugly. I could point out all day long things I didn't like about myself physically but if someone was to ask me to create a list of things I did like I'd have to cue the Jeopardy music because it'd take me a lunch break after an extended vacation to figure that out! What is a feature you love about yourself physically? For me, it's my smile. I paid good money (using my dad's insurance, of course) for my braces, and now, I have nice, straight teeth. I get complimented on my smile often, and I love flashing it. Yes, I'm pretty sure the average woman would love to lose that freshman 15 pounds she gained 12 years ago and I say go for it by maintaining a healthy lifestyle. However let's accept every inch of ourselves and learn to embrace the current beauty we have whatever this may be. I bet you can get lost in those beautiful eyes, them curves just keep going like the O in the alphabet, that skin is so silky like caress soap, oowwwww!! You're hot honey. The sooner you realize it the better.

Superhero evaluation questions to ask yourself:

- Do you feel as though you accept all parts of yourself?

- Go look in the mirror right now and do a full assessment. I challenge you to identity a minimum of three things you love about yourself internally and externally.

- Are there any other characteristics you can think of?

- Any talents you possess? Do you minimize these gifts? If so, how can you learn to appreciate them?

Chapter 16

Let It Go, Let It Gooo (Sing It with Me!)

Superwoman Leslie had a romantic relationship with a married man she met back in college. Now as a 37 year old mother of twin girls who are a product of this relationship, she feels very ashamed. However, he's the father of her children, and she feels as though she should remain in an uncomfortable situation for the sake of her girls.

Let's let people go who mean us no good right now. Don't pass go, don't collect $200 (yes I love Monopoly). Goodbye! Maybe that person is cheating on you, maybe they're hitting you-I hope not but maybe they haven't fully committed to you, you feel unappreciated, maybe they're verbally abusive or maybe that's just simply are not giving you the time and attention you so need and desire. I don't know but something in you is being pulled to say I don't want this anymore this is not for me. However we're holding on to it because we are scared to start over. Or you might say: Well we've been together for umpteen years, so what! Just because someone slaps you in your face every day for ten years and you've gotten to where the slaps don't hurt as much because you are accustomed to the daily pain doesn't mean you deserve to keep getting slapped in your face for another twenty years. See how silly that sounds! We are all so afraid to start over because we know our current demons and can control how to deal with the pain moderately. However, starting over may mean you get someone who makes you laugh, listens to you, appreciates you, and understands your boundaries. Ask yourself: What exactly am I holding onto? Is it the title, is it for appearance, is it financial because you can't afford to let this person go, maybe it's because you love them so much you don't know what life is like without them in it. But just because you love someone doesn't mean you're meant to be with them or it doesn't mean they are healthy for you. Also can you not love yourself more to put yourself in healthier situations? Will it hurt for you to let them go abso-freakin'-lutely! Will there be some sadness and uncomfortableness of being alone? Duh! But guess what you won't be mistreated, you won't be underappreciated, embarrassed or wishing for better because you'll be too busy working on better. Fearing the unknown is common, however sometimes it's the best thing you could have ever done. What if you're limiting yourself from something great? You can meet somebody tomorrow who has better intentions for you than someone you've known forever. Time means nothing character does!

Superhero evaluation questions to ask yourself:

- No one is perfect, but do you feel as though you are being respected and treated well? If not, what makes you stay?

- Do you use time to justify why you are staying in a situation you are uncomfortable with?

- Does the fear of the unknown scare you?

- Are you open to trying new things?

Chapter 17

There's A Reason the Rearview Mirror Is So Much Smaller Than the Front Windshield

Superwoman Amelia can't seem to get over her promiscuous past in college. She had a "reputation" and was known in her small town as the "yes woman." During the time, she proudly proclaimed she was free with her sexuality. However, later she grew embarrassed and relocated out of state for a new beginning. She avoids going to her alumni activities as she does not want anyone from her past to remind her of her old mentality. Her sorors tell her no one is concerned about it, but she feels self-conscious about taking the risk.

Have you ever noticed in your vehicle your rear-view mirror is super small compared to your front mirror when you're actually driving? That's because you only spend a very small fraction of your time backing up to look behind you with the gear in reverse. On the other hand you probably spend about ninety percent of your time looking forward with your gear in drive. We need to view our life with the same concept. We spend a lot of time and I mean a lot of time focusing on our past and what went wrong, how it hurt us, categorize things we haven't healed from, repeatedly review events in our lives we wish we could have done differently. The reality whether we like it or not is that it's done sis. No matter how good, bad and ugly it is or how much we don't want to accept it. There's nothing we can do about these life events. I know that's an easy thing to say when probably some of my most painful experiences are from the past. Rather, it's a bad childhood, relationship or whatever as I previously mentioned in my "Are We Damaged

Goods" chapter, so I don't want to go too deep into that. But I just really want you to think about how much time you spend in your car. You really don't spend a whole lot of time with your car in reverse because it's imperative to look forward to get to your destination safely. And so in that same token if you keep spending a lot of time in reverse, well you probably are going to wreck your car that you are still paying on, you probably are going have to swerve not to hit Toto your neighbor's dog (just kiddin I love animals). It just wouldn't be a good look for you to be driving in reverse. I need you to apply this philosophy to your life. You cannot live your life in reverse. You have to pay attention, focus on what you're doing, and drive forward past these speed bumps that have been difficult. I'm not saying forget it happened. I'm not saying you're aren't going to have an emotional reaction towards it when your mind goes there. I am saying limit the amount of time and energy you put on the reverse experiences. In my twenties I spent a lot of time really angry at my abuser. I spent a lot of time faulting that person and saying how my life could have been diffcrently and how it was negatively impacted by this person doing all these things to me and how I wanted to be vindicated because that person wasn't apologetic or they never gave me what I felt I needed to close that chapter. But I had to realize I was spending so much time focusing on those years of my childhood that I feel like I really wasn't living contently present-day. I really was glossing over all my blessings I had in my present life: I was a college graduate, a homeowner, eventually I did manage to find some good friends once I moved to Dallas, I was in good health, I was able to travel to see the world, I loved my career as a counselor helping others become mentally healthier. I had more than I imagined my adulthood would look like and yet somehow the biggest focus was my child abuse experiences. Now don't get me wrong that's something that is a very painful thing and I'm not trying to make light of it but I feel it was taking too much precedence over my life and I really had to shift my focus. I'm challenging you to do the same. Shift your focus. Maybe give yourself a time limit of how long you can think or feel about a certain subject. For example, I don't want to give that area more than 15 minutes of my time. If something triggers me and I think about, feel-get sad, mad or frustrated cool, fine so be it. But after 15 minutes, I need you to do something else to push past that moment. Now don't use my time frame as the end all be all. You may say hey Ashley I need a day or hey I need five hours. It doesn't matter. You know how long it is you need to get past the moment. I just want you to create a rule for your rear-view mirror experiences because we're not going to let these experiences and events have control over your life anymore. You're going to take control over the situation. Now I'm not trying to be all sunshine and roses here. This is not going to be an easy journey, so I don't want that to be misunderstood. But I do think it's something you can conquer. Right now, you're like a bull in a fine china shop, and I'm challenging you to be the bullfighter with the red flag. *"Ole'!"*

Superhero evaluation questions to ask yourself:

- Is there anything you feel you have been unable to get past?

- Are you avoiding this period in your life and/or continually reliving it?

- What do you think needs to happen in order for you to forgive yourself and/or accept your past?

- Are you taking the steps for this to happen? If not, what step would you like to start and when can you do it?

- How often will you evaluate if and when there is progression? Is there someone you feel comfortable enough to share with who can hold you accountable for taking action?

Chapter 18

Oops I spilled the milk on my carpet, let it sit and spoil or clean it up?

Superwoman Shara quit school and relocated 500 miles from her family for a relationship. However when her daughter was born her partner abruptly ended the relationship and no longer provided financial support for their child. Shara returned to her parents' house to help her figure out her next steps.

    How long do you cry over spilled milk? If you dropped a cup of milk on your carpet right now would you immediately find something to clean it up so that way it doesn't leave a stain and smell or would you look at it for three minutes saying I can't believe I dropped this milk, look at it running all over my floor? It would have tasted good too! It seems a little silly for you to do the latter correct? However we do so every day in our lives. We make mistakes, we think about what we should have, could have, would have been doing at this point in our lives, regret certain things and we keep replaying it over and over and over in our heads. Instead of cleaning up the mess and moving forward. How long are you going to beat yourself up about a choice(s) that you regret or person you dated or financial decision before you say okay let me clean this mess up? No you can't forget what happen but you can accept it for what it is, keep it real, heal, deal, and feel then keep it pushing.

Superhero evaluation questions to ask yourself:

- Is there an expiration date for your guilt?

- How long is too long to hold on to your past mishaps?

- What do you feel is needed for you to feel worthy of your own forgiveness?

Chapter 19

Damaged Goods, Or Can We Rebrand Ourselves?

Superwoman self/me: As I write this section of the book, I noticed a previously significant date on the calendar that recently passed May 11th, the day I met (and five years later married) my ex-husband. Let's set the scene: it's 2007 and I'd just graduated with my master's degree. So, I was feeling myself a little because in 2005 I'd obtained my bachelor's degree in three years flat. Two months post-graduation I was married to the guy I'd been dating for the last five years. So, yay me, two-time college grad, finally have a "real job" making good money as I've been told forever that's what I'm supposed to get and I'm definitely letting the world know on a regular basis I'm a Mrs. to a cutie patootie and aren't we just a nice profile pic couple? So, life is great since I've done all this by the age of 23, right? Hit the game buzzer: EEHHHHH, WRONG!!! A year later, we were divorced. I won't play blame game because I feel we both made some no no's in that year. To be honest neither of us had a true concept of what marriage meant and I think we were both just too immature to handle the hurdles that come with being someone's spouse. We aren't bad people we just weren't good together and I think we realized that once we said I do with the cute wedding pics and moved in together. We can talk today perfectly fine and have had many conversations about life post us and a few laughs at the blunder we called a marriage. But BABY back then I was devastated with a capital D!! I mean we went into this thing loudly belting out Chrisette Michele's a couple of forevers. This kind of thing isn't supposed to happen to me. I'm usually a person who does great in anything I set my mind too. I felt like a BIG FAT FAILURE!! I mean I'm divorced and I'm only 24. Now I try to awkwardly get back into dating having the slightest idea what I'm doing as I'd been dating him since I was 18. I'm thinking *girlfriend, you are totally damaged goods.* I mean who's going to want a divorcee and I can't believe I got it so wrong when it felt so right. It took me many and I do mean many years to work past this as I'd often cringe when I had to explain this failed marriage to friends, family and guys I dated (I didn't want to be dishonest when asked if I'd ever been married). So, I held onto to that badge of shame for years of this so called "mistake." But the question I had to ask myself is how long??? Seriously how long am I going to beat myself up over getting married too young, to the wrong person? How long am I going to be ashamed to speak about it? How long am I going to not forgive myself???? At some point do I get to rebrand, you know like the celebrities do or am I forever damaged goods?!?! For my spiritual and southern Christian folks please dust off your cup holders *excuse me* (cough cough) I mean bibles and turn with me to Luke 7:47 as it reads- "Therefore I tell you, her sins, many [as they are], are forgiven her — because she has loved much. But he who is forgiven little loves little." I'm going to steal a word from good ole Joel Osteen down in H-town hole it down-Did you know that forgiveness opens the door for love to operate in your life? Open your heart to forgiveness. Receive Christ's forgiveness and extend it to others. When you are forgiven much, you will love much. As Christ's love flows through you, your faith will be strengthened, your hope will be renewed, and you will be empowered to live the abundant life He has in store for you! Being in Christ comes with many benefits. You are a dearly loved, completely accepted, totally forgiven, uniquely chosen child of God. And because you have been adopted into God's family, you are now heir to a plethora of precious promises. So, we always talk about forgiving others but what about ourselves, why is that so hard to do??

Now I understand its 2019, and some folk aren't religious and are more spiritual, atheist, scientologist, heathen, etc. . Whatever floats your boat child cause I'm not here to judge and have a come one come all policy in my practice: I just want us all to be great!! So, for all that fit in the I don't have time to be reading them scriptures you are quoting category, the question is: Aren't you tired of staying in the 'damaged goods' section at the back of the grocery store? Don't you want to rebrand yourself? Now this is a lengthy little read ahead for those with a limited attention span like myself, but I promise at least one of the below examples applies to you:

So, you were a 304 back in the day and have a reputation at your college, small town, old job, or church. So freaking what! *(no pun intended-well, maybe a little bit!) You aren't one now, so how long are you going to hold your head down in shame? Have we learned nothing from Kim Kardashian? She took hoeing to new heights and rebranded it into a multimillion dollar business. And didn't Draya say a few years ago, "Your hoeness can be erased?" and might I add she also did a great job of making herself known for more than just being a groupie, lol? This isn't The Scarlet Letter so you don't need to have a big, fat "H" on all your Target clothes. There is life after hoeing, you know. You must move on and give yourself grace for not making the best choices in previous partners. Pray for forgiveness, go to counseling, see what made you so free with you goodies, if its self-esteem because they gave you attention then look for self-esteem building exercises to make sure you feel good about you and history doesn't repeat itself with your daughter(s) if you're now a mother. Look for attention in positive ways such as being a mentor, public speaking, acting/improv classes, being a lead or point person on the job, join your local urban league/NAACP and get involved. You have to start loving what you see in the mirror every day before you expect someone else to. If some guys treat you like you're still that chick from ten years ago, remember-a simple "no" won't hurt them. Seriously who cares what they think of you as they are not your husband. As hard as it is to hear, this type of guy may not ever take you serious besides that good lay in the sack as he's stuck on the past you, but someone else will so don't get so tore up over that one fool. He probably isn't that cute anyway if you turn your head to the side. I know many past "304 members" who canceled their memberships and are happily married today. And yes, they were transparent with their husbands/wives that their past wasn't squeaky clean and some even like that their partner "turns up" behind closed doors. Most importantly, let's not forget these guys gossiping about you-though they're paying none of your bills-so just keep them in your past honey and make a vow to yourself to be more stingy with your cookie in the future, use protection if you do share it and hold your head up high because you're a beautiful woman.*

Did you flunk out of school? So, what? Schools are open year-round, are even completely online now a days (University of Phoenix, Capella, Walden, etc.). It's never too late to go back. FAFSA can be obtained, they are giving student loans away like candy (but please use sparingly as you do have to pay them mugs back at some point unless you are part of a forgiveness program), you can research for local scholarships in your area, if you work for a major company see if your job has an educational reimbursement program. I see nontraditional students all the time accomplishing their goals. I saw a 95 year old woman named Ms. Nola on the internet getting her bachelor's degree so what's your excuse if Ms. Nola can strut her stuff on campus with that designer cane? If you happen to owe money that's stopping you from obtaining FAFSA, reach out to the school/collection agency to establish a payment plan or use those yearly taxes instead of possibly being colored and balling out on a new cell phone, car, or clothes you don't need to pay down the debt. If you don't have it like that make the sacrifice and set up a separate checking account for yourself to add money each paycheck to pay off the debt. No amount is too small when you are investing in yourself. If you learn differently or it takes you a bit longer to obtain the material maybe ask the school for accommodations for extended time, check into their tutoring hours and/or online tutoring.

You're a divorcee, or a relationship ended sourly even if it was mostly your fault? Ok, and…? If it's possible, have a conversation with that person to apologize and clear the air, if not pray to God for forgiveness and vow to do things differently moving forward. Or since it's 2019 and you and the Lord aren't cool like that, talk to yourself and have a conversation about what you took from this relationship. Be honest with your next partner and tell them you've learned from the error of your ways. Vow to be a nicer person, not to cheat, be more attentive, clean/cook more like your auntie used to do in the '70s for your favorite uncle, do those performances three nights a week that you saw on Pornhub, have more family time, whatever you declared you would try and seriously make an effort to do so. If you don't know how to do something, ask someone you feel comfortable with for tips or look online for articles to help. The internet has it all.

You made some really jacked up financial decisions: credit score number is now looking like your water bill, none of your people trust you enough to loan you money because they will never see it again, you don't have a retirement account, no savings, are living check to check, you owe some bill collectors and you had to change your number to duck and dodge them? Um, ok-you know you can fix your credit, right? People do it all the time. If you know financial literacy is foreign to you reach out to professionals. Most of your jobs have an employee assistance program that allows you to consult with a financial advisor for free, there are tons of free apps that help you keep track of your finances, websites such as http://www.practicalmoneyskills.com/resources/free materials that can give you resources, most churches offer free financial classes or if that makes your butt itch to step in the holy place check your local community center for free financial resources. Also, the guru Dave Ramsey has awesome books on getting rid of debt https://www.daveramsey.com/. Credit Karma is also a good free place to start. Reach out to at least one of those collections agencies and see if you can create a payment plan to get it off your credit, try to auto draft $20 per paycheck minimum into a savings account, if you get paid biweekly that's $520 a year. Ally bank www.ally.com allows you to open an account for free without any balance, and if you have direct deposit, you can set it automatically to go into this account that you don't have easy access to and prevent yourself from blowing the money. If you owe your cousin Ray Ray, maybe try to give him a few dollars-even if it has been two years later. Point is, you have to start somewhere just don't stay stagnant! Some progress is better than no progress. Don't convince yourself that since it's not happening all at once there's no point. A snail still reaches his destination eventually, right?

Got fired from a job? You do know they have other employers right?! If you live in a major city you pass by corporate offices every day. I know that job made your ego feel great and it was a bit of a blow to no longer have that as part of your identity, but don't you have more to offer in your greatness besides them 40 hours for someone else's company?! And yes, we all need money to pay our bills so get back in the grove. Even though job searching is a full-time job itself you can do it! Go to networking events and bump elbows with the who's who in your area, ask your family and friends if their company is hiring and let them know you are looking, are you part of an alumni association with your school? If so reach out to them. I mean that's what you pay fifty dollars a year for, the perks! If you are in a sorority time to Order of Eastern Star, skee-wee, ooo-oop, z phi and eee yip towards a job HUNTY. That's just what sorors are supposed to do-help each other out! You better get off your high horse and ask them can they hook you up pink, red, blue, and gold style. Somebody in that grad chapter works in or knows HR, update your resume and linked in profile and make sure you have given copies out, go to that local job fair, register with the workforce center or temp agencies and follow up biweekly, Hire a head hunter to market you, Or maybe it's time to start that business you've always dreamed of. Point is, when you die, your obituary is not going to say employee number___, so why put so much stock into that position? Stop feeling bad because it didn't work out and move on to bigger and better!

You played the side chick or had a child out of wedlock and embarrassingly did the Maury you are not the father once or twice to figure out some things. It's ok. You love your child and they are in a healthy stable environment. Besides, when your son/daughter looks at you with those big cute eyes all they have is unconditional love. They could care less about how they got here or your past indiscretions. They simply see the best mom in the world. If you don't feel you are/were the best parent. It's not too late: take a parenting class, reach out to an elder in your family for advice on how to do things differently, or if your kids are old enough ask them what they'd like you to work on. If you are/were side-chicking it up, no judgment here but ask yourself why you're ok with being in the number two slot and how long this will work for you. If it's already over then at some point you have to-you already know the word

forgive *yourself for messing up someone else's covenant. If you're bold enough then maybe an apology to the spouse is an option, if not, then you have to just make a vow to block that person from your life and not go back down that rabbit hole. Most men don't leave their wives or baby mommas for the side chick. And in the event they do then guess what your side chick spot is now open so like my granny used to say "you may lose him how you get him." Idk if it's true but definitely something to ponder on. If you're past that side chick life then coparent if you guys are in that boat and let that be the end all be all. Go after that gold medal which is the number one spot as you were never meant to be second class. No one sets out for the silver in the Olympics.*

You did someone wrong and disappointed someone such as a parent, friend, boyfriend/girlfriend, or soror and you've felt guilty since. If they are willing to talk to you, then maybe it's time to face the music, apologize, and discuss ways to rebuild the relationship/reestablish trust. Are you bold enough to write them a letter if you don't feel comfortable putting yourself out there face-to-face? Or come up with one-two things you can do to show your regrets as you know the person and what they like. If they have totally written you off, as much it hurts, you have to forgive yourself at some point and move on with the promise not to hurt another person in the same way. Don't continue to be that person with bad character that people warn others about. There is life after petty.

So, you had previous substance abuse issues. Maybe it's best to stay away from people and places that trigger you. Know your limits. AA/NA groups work for some and others it doesn't but maybe you should consider starting a hobby, volunteer in some way that holds you accountable such as mentoring, establishing a nursing home friendship as they are often lonely and their families don't visit, teach a class at the homeless shelter, start a food drive/feed the needy, start a scholarship in your area for kids with financial need, something whereas if your presence is missed someone is going to ask why you aren't around. If that's not your calling, then ask yourself what is. Point is, stay busy and active. If y'all can't tell, I'm good and southern, but the saying goes: "An idle mind is the devil's workshop." I think there's a bit of truth to that even without the religious connotation. Surround yourself with a good support group. And if you have that urge, better let it be known and come up with some realistic coping strategies to help you stay clean. Easier said than done for sure, but worth a try.

I'm going to put all jokes aside on this topic as it's very sensitive and many women struggle with guilt and shame after making this decision. You had an abortion(s) before. Maybe you were too young to rear a child, you couldn't afford to care for a baby, it was the wrong guy to coparent with, you didn't want to disappoint your family, maybe your religious beliefs conflict with this choice and so on. I don't care if you are prochoice, anti, prolife, abortion is a hard decision period! *A lot of women feel ashamed and guilty after and suffer in silence as abortion is a hot topic, meaning* everyone *has an opinion on it and some women just don't want to hear the shame on you for having one speech. But sis you can't continue to suffer in silence. You need to be honest about how you feel as not acknowledging this is an unhealthy coping style. And let me also add its ok to mourn your baby even if you know it was for the best to proceed with the abortion. It's still a loss and don't let anyone tell you what and how you should feel. I want you to be unapologetically honest about how your emotions. If you get sad around the time of the baby's due date, acknowledge that. If it's anger that the child's father seemed unfazed by your decision acknowledge that and so on. Point is be real so you can heal. Know your triggers and how to deal with them if/when they should arise. For example, if seeing other pregnant women is a trigger for thinking negatively about the abortion, then identify a positive way of coping with this situation. Everyone knows at least one person that's had an abortion. Now again I'm not stating whether I agree or disagree as that's irrelevant. I am saying it's common so maybe reaching out to someone for support. If you belong to a church and you know they are a loving and nonjudgmental group maybe consulting with a member/asking for bible verses and prayers to help you cope. Keep a journal if you don't feel comfortable talking to someone you know or here's a non-judgmental and supportive resource: 1-866-4-EXHALE or http://www.yourbackline.org.*

Fell off on your relationship with God if you are a believer? It's never too late to reconnect. There's a church on every corner in the south, lol, so just play "eenie meenie miney moe" and pick one, I'm sure your granny, aunt, or mom would love to do a show and tell on their heathen relative that returned to the House of the Lord and cook you a nice Sunday dinner afterward (smile I'm just teasing). Or if you can't stomach being on display at your childhood church and too much messiness is still going on since you just know Deacon Jones is over Sister Smith's house more than just for bible study (jokes people, relax) most mega churches have online sermons, you can call in anonymously for prayer on that good old Morning Prayer line, google daily/weekly lessons, many free apps you can download will send you inspirational quotes, or start your own life group with friends. Point is don't let guilt stop you from restarting.

This is the year of renewal and rebranding. We will not continue to allow our past to dictate our future. Don't be what I call an IMA girl- I'ma do this this and that but never start. Don't *talk* about it, *be* about it! Whatever's on your heart, do it! Your past isn't squeaky clean? So, what? No one really has a picture perfect life. Some are just better at hiding their dirt than others. Unfortunately for you yours was just a bit more public but *trust,* everyone has a few skeletons in their closet. So, don't let your damaged past make you think you'll have a jacked up damaged future. Hit that Aaliyah- "If at first you don't succeed, dust yourself off and try again." Put it on repeat and go!

Chapter 20

Shoulda, Coulda, Woulda

Superwoman Remy thinks daily on how she is failing herself in not meeting her personal goals. She has a never ending list of expectations she has not yet accomplished. She feels at her age she needs to be further along. Her thoughts go something like this

I should be married
I should have kids
I should read a book(s)
I should find a church home
I should be finished with my degree by now
I should own a house by now
I should have known about financial literacy and/or made better financial decisions
I should have traveled to _____
I should have been less promiscuous
I shouldn't have been friends with that person
I shouldn't have moved to this area
I should lose more weight or look like…
I should have accepted that job
I would be happier if this had/hadn't happened to me

Sound familiar? Get rid of the following statements: *I should be, I should have by now, compare to so-and-so, I'm not at the place I want to be, I always, I never, I'm not good at it, I'm horrible at it, I can't, I don't look right.* Replace the "should of, could of, would of" with: I would like to, I am going to work towards, I will set a goal to do___, and reevaluate in ___ amount of time.

'Should' suggests 'ought to,' which can make what we are intending to do feel like a chore. 'Could' is a positive word; it expresses possibility-a version of 'can,' -we have the power. All things are possible with 'could.' Using 'could' instead of 'should' aligns with our choices and possibilities. It may inspire us to pursue our desires, but 'should' falls just short of overbearing obligation.

Training Your Brain to Use Could Over Should When You Think

Own your thoughts-The next time you hear yourself saying you 'should' do something, take a minute to ask yourself why this is important. Is it something you want bad enough or are you telling yourself you want it because you think it's what is supposed to be right? If it's because you think it's supposed to be important, then remove it from your mind completely and own up to what you truly want.

Mark a line through it and cancel it- cancel out negative words. Anytime you hear yourself using 'should' for example, quickly repeat over and over 'cancel, cancel, cancel." Don't let your negative thinking get the best of you; replace the negative with a 'cancel."

Believe you can make it happen. The moment you believe you can, you will be amazed by your strength to fight any situation you find yourself in. When you're looking at your "coulds," you need to really believe you can. Put a plan in action to help you achieve your goals. What do you need to do in order to make them happen?

Superhero evaluation questions to ask yourself:

- What is your definition of enough as it's hard to judge yourself when you don't have a true measurement of knowing what makes you feel content?

- If you had all of the things you feel you are missing would that be enough or would you diminish the accomplishment(s) and immediately think of a new goal or thing missing from your life?

Chapter 21

Ignorance Isn't Bliss

Superwoman Xiomara has considered designing dresses and opening a consignment shop. However, she does not know how to go about opening her own business, nor is she familiar with anyone is this industry.

Ignorance is, simply put, the lack of knowledge. For me a person who struggled for many years with their self-esteem one of the most paralyzing feelings is not knowing/understanding something. You know in your mind you want to start something, you wish you could do something or accomplish certain things like other people do but you have no idea how they even begin that because it's so outside of your area of expertise and because you don't want to look like boo boo the fool (that's what all black Mama's say) you'd rather not take that chance and stay in the known versus taking the risks and it possibly not going the way you thought it would go. We are so scared of people knowing that we don't know something but we have to really think that somebody had to start that thing we desire to do, had to do a trial-and-error phase in order for them to become a subject matter expert, for them to write that book, for them to put the information online, on YouTube, or for them to be on TV and give advice they had to fuck it up for lack of better words so many times before they got it right. So, my question to you is are you willing to "fuck it up" a couple or possibly many times before you get it? We are in the technology era. If we don't know something that's what the World Wide Web is for. I know it's a bit prehistoric, but there is a library in every major city-and it's filled with books that give you information to do that very thing you want to do.

YouTube has everything online for someone who's done that area you're interested in. I've even seen on social media nowadays where people advertise their services to say you can pay them to Mentor you. Or you can go old-school and break out that phone book and cold call those people in your area who do what you want to do and ask them if you pay for lunch would they be willing to lend you an hour for you to ask questions about what they do now. Keep in mind you're going to get a few "no's" before you get a 'yes,' so don't let that deter you. Keep pushing until somebody says yes. The point I'm trying to make it is we cannot allow our false perception of our self-doubt to stop us from gaining the knowledge we wish to obain. It's not as embarrassing as you think being in the unknown because half the people who are pretending to know don't know diddly. They're just putting on a front because they don't want you to realize they are just as ignorant in the area as you are. Somebody has to stop acting and start knowing. Why not let that be you?

Superhero evaluation questions to ask yourself:

- Would you be willing to write down your concerns, fears, questions, things you don't know, etc.?

- Once this is finished, how much time per day could you dedicate to educating yourself?

- Are you ok with admitting to others you have little to no knowledge on a subject?

- Are you ok with things not going as you planned the first go around?

- Does a possible 'no' stop you from pursuing your goals?

Chapter 22

Unnnnhh, No Limits Baby

Superwoman Reagan considered planning an event for a fundraiser for her local community. However, she limited the event to 100 people just in case only half of that showed up-even though she invited 350 and the location can hold 500.

Why do we say well I want to apply for that position but insert limit, I want to start that business but maybe I shouldn't, I'm not quite sure if I'll do well insert limit, maybe I should just be happy where I am maybe I shouldn't say I'm unhappy with insert limit, what will people think if I tell them I want to do this/I want to start this/I want to try this? Other questions: what if I fail what if I'm not good at it insert a thousand other limits. We place these roofs on ourselves on how far we think we should reach. But who said it is set in stone that we can only go so far? The only difference between you and that celebrity mogul you admire is they took the cap off the lid. What I mean by that is they kept trying, and even when they failed, they didn't let what somebody else said about what they couldn't do deter them. When there was no lane, they bought the bricks, gravel, and shovel from *Lowe's* and made one. They put in the hard work, they didn't let the cries that came from the pain in building and strengthening their muscles stop them. What if Queen Bey let a certain gaudy fashion line in the late 90s early 2000's get her down? Then we wouldn't have the park that is Ivy, honey. She learned from her mistakes, modified, and improved! She didn't throw a pity party and say, "Well, I didn't do as well as I envisioned, so I guess I'll never try that again." And let me point out that she is a singer and dancer-not a fashion designer. Well she *was* only that, but now you better put some *respect* on Mrs. Carters name! *Now* she's a fashion designer. And what about Auntie Oprah? Before her, what African-American woman you know had her own talk show or was a billionaire building schools in Africa? The point I'm trying to make is your possibilities are limitless. You have no ceiling! Don't limit yourself to what somebody said you can do, and don't limit yourself to see what somebody says you can't be. Just because the idea is not popular at the moment and seems very difficult to make happen doesn't mean it can't happen. I had so many people tell me certain things about how I should limit my success and myself once I reached a certain level professionally and personally. They told me I'm doing too much, and I shouldn't overextend myself. How can they tell me what's best for me? Nobody knows me like I know myself, so if I feel like I can keep pushing, try a new business venture, move to another city, or start working on another project, why would I let somebody else tell me what's enough for me? If it came into my mind and I felt like I could do it, why would I doubt that "try it" spirit just because someone else told me to slow down? Do you know how silly it sounds for someone else to tell you how much success you can obtain because he/she hasn't obtained success or was too scared to even try? What you want to dream is between you and God but no one else. I don't think people mean it to be malicious. I just think people have limits on themselves and they in turn project those limitations on you. But it's your responsibility to let that slide off your back, keep grinding and push past those road blocks. I don't know which of these if any apply to you: maybe you want a new job, to move to a new city, purchase a home, travel, join a new organization, start a new relationship, invent something, whatever but go for it!! Don't even go back and forth trying to run it by your people. If it feels right in your spirit, go for it as long as you can live with the consequences that occur from that decision-good, bad, or indifferent. Remember there is not elevator to success. You have to take the stairs, but the view is always pretty at the top.

Superhero evaluation questions to ask yourself:

- Do you tell your vision to others hoping they will share in your aspiration?

- Does it deter you if they aren't as excited or don't feel what you want to do is a good idea?

- Do you feel you have any limits on your life right now? If so what are they?

- Do you feel you can remove any? If so, why or why not?

- Why did you place the limitations on yourself to begin with?

- Are you willing to start small or does it have to be big for you to feel it is worthy of your energy?

Chapter 23

Like Nike, Just Do It!

Superwoman Brooklyn has a habit of making plans she doesn't follow through on. She has good intentions, but her friends take what she says with a grain of salt as she is not known to be a woman of her word. She's described as being "flaky."

I call folks "Imas" when they are always "bumping their gums" about imaginary goals but have no "Action Jackson" in them. These are the one that'll say, "I'ma go to school next semester," but haven't registered for even one class and have no major. Or, "I'ma look for a new job," but they haven't updated their resume or applied for any new positions within or outside of their company. Then there's the, "I'ma move to another city because I'm tired of living in a small one," but they can't say when they are planning this adventure and they haven't researched the cost of living in the desired area nor saved money for the move. Here's another, "I'ma get back active in the sorority," but haven't gone to any meetings nor researched the local chapter smh. Are you an "I'ma" woman? Do you talk a lot about what you are going to do, plan to do, or want to do, but don't? Do you make false promises to your friends? Sis, you can't keep being that person people don't take seriously when she opens her mouth-so let's set some goals, deadlines, and have some sort of accountability system here. Things need to be written down and specific-not in your head and vague. Your days are long, but your years are short. You don't want to look back one day and have nothing to show for your life. Make it count.

1. Book that trip you've wanted to take! Or at least set a deadline and save money from each paycheck to go toward that dream vacation.
2. Look into furthering your education if you desire to do so.
3. That sorority you want to join and/or get back active in? Go see when the membership intake is or when the reclamation period starts.
4. That restaurant you've been wanting to try? Go do it! Set a lunch or dinner date with someone.
5. That business you've been wanting to start? Do it! Work on this every week. Stay consistent.
6. Work out and lose weight so you feel comfortable with yourself. I would say get serious about your weight loss and eating habits-don't just join a gym and waste $30 each month. Find group workouts, get a partner, set a goal to lose weight/inches in a reasonable time, cook rather than eat out, track those calories with Fitbit, etc.

As you know, I can go on forever about the "I'mas," but I won't. I just really want you to say what you mean and mean what you say moving forward.

Superhero evaluation questions to ask yourself:

- Why is it difficult for you to follow through on plans you make?

- Do you feel as though you overextend yourself?

- Is your time management off?

- Do you set too many goals in an unrealistic timeframe?

- Does it affect you any being known as the person who "just talks" but is not about action?

Chapter 24

Speak, Know, Do

Superwoman Hazel is a sophomore in college who desires to start a fashion line. She often makes clothes for herself and receives many compliments on them. She decided to put her designs on display at a booth for a local festival, but she only sold one of her items and now feels as though she is not meant to be a designer and should not further pursue her desire.

Say what you want to accomplish out loud-don't just think it. Once you say it, write it down. Then, ask yourself, "How can I work to make that happen with my daily actions?" If you don't know then that's when you figure out your game plan on how to educate yourself to make it a reality. Ask around as somebody has to be able to point you in the right direction. I'm not saying it's going to be easy, I'm not saying you going to get it all the way right the first time, but I do believe when you know better you do better. So that's your mission: to figure out how to know how to get that thing(s) you said you wanted and that doesn't land in your lap or is delivered to you via Amazon Prime in two days. You must put in the work to make it a reality. Nobody's going to give you anything. It also doesn't matter if your friend Susie and Keisha had a two-parent household, disposable income, multiple resources, great support system and that's not your situation. So, what? It could still happen for you, but you have to be willing to put in that work. Are you willing to hustle? Are you really in the grind until it becomes a reality and everything you thought of comes to fruition? You may say to yourself, *Ashley, that's easy for you to say, but I don't have XYZ. I don't have money, and I don't have time.* Again, you can't deposit excuses. If you want it hard enough is yours. Faith without works is dead so you must put in at work. If you aren't willing to work for it, don't complain about not having it. People pray for cake, and then when God gives them butter, eggs, oil, a pan and an oven, they get frustrated and leave the kitchen. Ask yourself whether you're willing to demand transformation or settle for what's easy. Remember doubts kill more dreams than any failures ever will.

You don't plant the seed and eat the fruit the same day. Meaning sometimes we have to stop getting frustrated that we aren't progressing at microwave speed. That's not reality. When you plant a flower, fruit, or vegetable you have to water it to make sure you keep the weeds out and patiently wait for it to grow so you can eat it. But you also have to know that you can't expect it to happen all in one day. It's the same concept in business. It's not going to be perfect the first day you open the doors. You're not going to make as much money as you think you should as soon as you graduate from college. The moment you decide to get your life right spiritually does it mean that your life magically falls in the place? Probably not. You're still going to have temptation. If you're trying to work on communication in a relationship it doesn't mean you guys are going to never argue and so on and so on. Have patience in your journey. People often romanticize their plans but realize the execution and magic you are looking for is in the work you're avoiding. There's no other way around it. When you look on social media and see these successful people you have to think about all the behind-the-scenes crying, frustration, disappointment, doubt, and fear, involved to keep them pushing to make their dream a reality

Superhero evaluation questions to ask yourself:

- Do you feel as though you are speaking confidence or planting seeds of doubt into your life's journey? If the latter, is that something you'd like to go about differently? Name 3 ways to do so?

- Do you feel as though you are thoroughly knowledgeable on how to obtain what you desire? If not, how are you going to increase your awareness on the topic?

- Do you feel as though you have a realistic timeframe on how to make what you want a reality, or do you feel as though you are romanticizing the outcome?

Chapter 25

Poison, Poison (Queue BelBivDevoe)

Superwoman Isis spends a lot of time with her cousin who is three months younger than her. Isis feels as though her cousin lives a certain lifestyle that's a bit overwhelming-and sometimes has her in illegal situations she is not comfortable being involved in. However, she's family, so she often goes along to get along.

Sometimes people have job titles with no job duties/responsibilities. Sometimes we get caught up on well that's my mom, sister, cousin etc. but they don't meet the expectations or take on the responsibility of that title. Ask yourself title removed if you'd be friends with or allow this person in your life if you met them now?

These people sap more energy than a mosquito from Louisiana at a cookout in July. They can be taxing on your mental health/peace, they don't have boundaries and often are easy to spot out. What are signs of toxic people in your life?

- They only call you when they need something but ghost you when you are asking for that same financial or emotional support
- They are judgmental. I mean they really know how to kick your self-esteem in the balls by bringing up that mistake you made in 1979 every time they see you
- They have more drama than a *Love and Hip-Hop* episode. They are drawn to it like a moth to a flame fueled by the fire (big ups to Janet Jackson, if you don't know that song, you're either too old or too young *[face palm]*).

- They gaslight you. If your family member continually claims they never said something, when you and everyone else knows they did, it might not seem that serious. However, this is a form of gaslighting, which is highly emotionally abusive behavior.
- They flip-flop between positive and negative reinforcement. They can lash out at you, yell and insult you. However, once you ignore them after this senseless attack, they'll likely coax you back into their trap by offering you pseudo-praise and support. Typically, these positive interactions are short-lived before this individual goes back to their typical manipulative behavior.

You find yourself explaining over and over or trying to convince this person what they're doing is emotionally harmful to you, yet they don't change their behavior and words. No matter who this person is in your life you have to ultimately decide if the relationship is worth the agony. If so, establish very hard core boundaries. Yes, I realize this will be uncomfortable for you and the other party may not like the fact that you aren't as lenient as you once were. But point blank you have to protect your emotional wellbeing. You may be uncertain on how the person will react, if this will affect the dynamics of relationship, experience some guilt, nor be familiar with what boundaries you want to set, or need a second to recover from such an emotionally abusive relationship but move forward anyway. *Yes,* I said emotionally abusive. Sometimes toxic people make it seem as though it's not that bad or you are overreacting, but this is part of the abuse.

Superhero evaluation questions to ask yourself:

- What is your definition of healthy vs unhealthy relationships? Using this definition, what category do you feel the people in your life fall in?

- Do you have any people in your life you are holding on to due to their possible title (cousin, friend since fourth grade, parent, etc.) that you don't feel are healthy for you to be around?

- Do these people leave you drained after being around them for extended periods of time?

- Ask yourself when has too much poison ever helped anyone in any way?

- Evaluate how you can modify this relationship where it's a bit on the healthier side. If you can't think of anything, ask yourself why this relationship is still occurring and whether it's in your best interest to continue?

- What is preventing you from ending and/or limiting your time with these individuals? Would you feel guilty if you did so? Why or why not?

Chapter 26

GASLIGHTING Without the Match

Superwoman Youna has been in a relationship with Lola for the past year. Youna does not like the tone Lola uses with her. But whenever she expresses this to Lola, she informs her she is being too sensitive and making a bigger deal out of things than needs be. Youna then starts to question herself and whether she should bring up times where she is uncomfortable to Lola.

Gaslighting is a very sneaky form of emotional abuse. When you have a chance, you should Google the formal definition of it. If I had to sum it up fairly quickly I'd say it's brainwashing at its finest. It's a tactic people use on you to make you question your perception as if it's not reality. It's a way for people to have control over your emotions by denying or avoiding accountability for their actions. Have you ever had conversations with people where they've said or done things to you they've conveniently forgotten, or they remember the conversation totally different from how it really went as if you guys weren't in the same room talking about the same thing? They really make you question your sanity and if the conversation even happened (or sometimes they'll actually say the conversation didn't happen) as though you made it up. Gas lighters are very charming and convincing people so they do a really good job of making you question whether you are being too sensitive, rather it didn't happen the way you thought it happened, make you feel that you're wrong or give you that guilty nagging feeling for even bringing up something that bothered your peace of mind. They also have a way of using love and flattery as a hidden agenda to justify or explain their actions, possibly even discrepancies in their communication to shoe under a rug your grievances. This temporarily makes you feel reassured. However you ignore your gut and get so confused, that what you even came to them for in the first place may have been silly only to wash and repeat later because again these persistent Little Liars strike multiple times not just once. You'll even get those ones who act surprised and hurt that you would even suspect them of treating you wrong. They will flip it on you and accuse you of being (insert adjective like insecure, overly sensitive), question your intellect, say you are aggressive and have anger issues ETC. . These are very sophisticated bullies. Gaslighting can take place in any kind of relationship. It could be your family, it could be friends, it could be romantic and typically these are the hardest ones to confront because we care about these people so much and we don't want to believe they would treat mistreat us.

The longer gaslighting lasts/has been going on the harder it is for you to take control of it because the individual is really pushing the agenda that you're stinky perceptions are severely off, until the more you doubt and the less likely you are to say something to that person or stop the current communication because you're thinking well that's just them. I've had this conversation before, maybe I am being too sensitive. It really does a number on your self-esteem and your confidence. Again, it's a sneaky form of verbal abuse. It's not in your face like someone cursing you out and/or using vulgar language. This one makes you judge and blame yourself for someone else's actions. Imagine the irony in that. You have to learn the gas lighters patterns and recognize how you go about challenging and recovering from the gaslighting. You have to validate your reality. Don't get caught up in the insecurities or shame that someone else duped you for lack of better words. Acknowledge what the real deal is versus what they're telling you so that way you can decipher through the fiction and a facts. Also surround yourself around other people because isolation only heightens gaslighting. Don't take it personal. You're not the first and you're not going to be the last person they gaslight so don't question their methods and ask/say why did I deserve that and what did you/I do wrong that this person didn't care about me enough to value our relationship? I'm pretty confident this person is gaslighting as many people as possible present day. They do not care who it is as long as they get what they want because these people have selfish personalities.

Here are a few signs of gaslighting:

1. Their car is parked on Denial Drive. You know something was said/done. They know it, too, but they will swear on a stack of bibles it didn't happen-which makes you question yourself. Remember, their goal is for you to accept their perception and make it your reality.

2. What's important to you they use against you and attack the core of who you are. For example, say you enjoy singing. They'll tell you that you'd be a good singer if you sounded more like a certain artist, or if you modified your style it'd maybe be better. They will give you a compliment and insult at the same time to make you doubt your awesomeness. It's so confusing and mentally draining to decipher their motives. When they compliment you, it makes you think, *well, they are ok, they aren't that bad*, but newsflash-they *are that bad*! On the flip side, when they insult you that uneasy feeling comes back and you're wondering occasionally if the praise is authentic. That may be gaslighted as well. TEW Much right!

3. They are persistent people, so they have the time to wear you down to exactly where they want you to be. They mold you gradually and once they have a groove, they up the ante. It's like climbing a hill with a slight incline. When you are climbing it doesn't seem like you've inclined much but after about a mile or 20 minutes of walking you look back and realize how elevated you are.

4. They are a regular old Pinocchio, they wouldn't know the truth if it fell in their lap gift wrapped.

5. People's actions don't match their words. Who cares what they are telling you, sis-watch how they are treating you.

6. Confusion is a distraction-most people value stability and normality. A gas lighter's biggest strength/weapon is to confuse you by blurring what reality is and have you questioning half the things you are thinking, feeling and/or seeing. We look for others to help us stabilize when we are feeling unstable. The gas lighter is waiting to be put in the game to be that person you depend on because they've caused so much instability in your mind and when they do, they have just hit the jackpot. Now they know their power has been activated thus they have a lotus of control of you.

7. The old switcheroo. They point the finger. They are the culprit here yet pin the bad guy label on you. It gets to a point where they accuse you so often you find yourself defending your character and get distracted from the original behavior the gas lighter presented that you despised and originally addressed.

8. Homie love-they will fake use people against you. They'll have an imaginary team of people they "claim" agree with them no matter what and are coincidentally in disagreement with you. But funny thing is you've never actually heard these people agree with the gas lighter. They are just relaying the message that you are supposedly wrong. Keep in mind a gas lighter lies for their own benefit, so if they have to pit you and a few friends against each other than so be it. It makes you question the other parties involved and if they are trustworthy/do they dislike you. And if you are backing away from the crew well then that means you are isolating and more likely to talk to the gas lighter only and that's what they want.

9. They are extremely dismissive and want you to question your sanity.

10. They also don't want others believing they are gas lighters. Again, they prefer to be sneaky. Keep your eyes and ears open

Superhero evaluation questions to ask yourself:

- Now that you know the signs of a gaslighters, what can you do to start protecting yourself without the false guilt?

- Are you prepared to stand your ground to a gas lighter once he/she gives resistance to what you need/want to continue communication?

Chapter 27

Meeting People Where They Are

Superwoman Raleigh's dad has been inconsistently in and out of her life since her birth. Every time he makes a surprise pop up visit he makes broken promises. Whenever her father doesn't do as he initially agreed she finds herself really upset and disappointed.

Are the expectations we set in our mind realistically in line with who the person has shown us he or she is time after time again? Sometimes we get so caught up in what we want the person to do/be. But has that person ever shown you they can meet and/or are even capable of meeting this expectation?

The Difference Between Accepting and Respecting

You can accept that someone is more mixed up with nuts than trail mix but that doesn't mean you have to put up with them disrespecting you.

Sometimes we have to discern between the box we created somebody to fit in and the circle they really are in. Maybe because I'm a counselor, but I have a bad habit of looking at people's potential and how great I think they can be. I have a fairytale vision of unlimited greatness that I feel overshadows where the individual(s) currently are. It's a grossly unfair disadvantage to the person because I have this high expectation for them and when they don't meet it, I have the nerve to be frustrated. However, they never agreed to be that person. In fact they showed me who they were initially, yet I just chose to ignore it. Yes it's disappointing when people aren't who you think, assume or want them to be. But it's even more disappointing when you continue to place an unrealistic expectation on them, and they continue to miss the mark. When someone shows you who they are, there's no if, ands, or buts about it-you have to take them at face value and say: "Okay, this is what I have. Do I want to take it or leave it, not edit, but accept it or not?" Unrealistic expectations are unhealthy and damaging because they set everybody up for failure. A question I want you to ponder is if you have unrealistic expectations for the people in your life? If so, identify all the expectations you have for this person. Maybe write it/them down. Be honest and put down all those things you have expectations on because it's important for you to recognize what they are. Once you've finished your list I need you to go through it and scratch off things that you haven't a hundred percent done yourself because surely if is unrealistic for you how can we expect somebody else to do it? Let's say for instance you still have many things on the list that you are 100% committed to because you're like well I did do all those things on those lists Ashley because *"I'm a good person."* Just because you can do all these things and live up to meet certain expectations doesn't mean somebody else can sunshine. So you have to honestly know who you're dealing with. For example I don't have a great relationship with someone in my immediate family. I don't think I ever will just because of our personalities, and I had come to terms with that. It doesn't matter if I strongly want it or don't want it and no matter how much I tried to force it in the past it just wasn't happening. I have to know now that person's personality and my personality are like oil and water-it just doesn't mix! Yes, I do recognize my desire and my previous expectations didn't align which is what led me to come to terms with what it was and wasn't going to be.

It seems that most people get caught up in just one gesture from another person they are interested in. Like when someone gives that one special gift or does that wonderful thing for you that one time. That does not mean that's who they are. That's probably was just something done singularly. This false perception hurts people from seeing the hard core truth at times of who they are truthfully dealing with. For example, seeing a person in the gym or walking for exercise. Just because you come across that person that one time does not mean that's something they do "all the time." It's just the moment you reacted to this person they're in the environment or state. What if the person you saw in the gym exercising was on day one of their *new year new me kick* and didn't return to the gym for another month? Can we really say they are consistently exercising? No, you just coincidently caught them on a good day. I hear people say often that "he's really a nice guy" or "she's not really like that" still hanging on to one moment they think is the core of that person, but it is not. That's why so many people want to give themselves time before making any serious moves. People need to let the dust settle and give things time to really see if individuals are who they say they are and not who you wish they are. We do a bad job sometimes at questioning people regarding their intention and usually have to start wait on their actions as the tell tell of the truth. I see people that I believe have great potential all the time. However, I've been down the road of trying to get them to see that light and their bill is not paid. The light is not coming on, so I just meet them where they are. All people don't want what I do or might not be as brave, so I accept them where they are regardless of my desire for them.

Superhero evaluation questions to ask yourself:

- Do you know the difference between desires and expectations?

- Do you feel your expectations for some people are realistic or a pipe dream?

- Do you feel as though how you want a person to be is in alignment with who they actually are?

- In order to limit your frustrations/disappointments do you feel you need to realign your expectations to who the person is consistently showing you they are verses who you desire them to be?

- Can you come up with 3 modified expectations for the individuals that comes to mind that you are not meeting where he/she is?

Chapter 28

Why Are You Asking Why?

Superwoman Janelle has been in a relationship for almost two years. The person she is involved with cheats, speaks disrespectfully and does not seem concerned about her feelings. She is often wondering why this individual doesn't love her the way she desires and what she did to deserve this type of relationship.

Why are you negotiating on how a person is going to respect you? Why ask why a person didn't meet your expectations to say/do things for you or not say and do what you like? And even if you did get the full details on why they acted an idiot would it change the disappointment and hurt you feel from how they treated you? Sometimes there's not a logical reason why people say or do or don't say or do what you think they should have, could have, would and could have to be in your life. Sometimes you're not meant to understand the foolishness of other people but why keep repeating, explaining and negotiating on the treatment you know you deserve? If that person is past the age of 18 years old then chances are they probably have good comprehension skills and deductive reasoning. If they don't evaluate why you are spending so much time explaining yourself to someone who is not the sharpest knife in the kitchen drawer. So, let's set a new rule that if they don't get you after that second or third time you effectively communicate your major needs/desires maybe it's time to reevaluate if they deserve a spot in your life. It's not so hard for them to understand what they want, you're not a difficult person nor is what you're asking too much. Maybe they're just giving too little honey.

Regardless if they don't want to put in the effort to give what you are asking for because of character flaws, lack of respect and/or they are just a shitty person none of that is your business to figure out the reason why. But you can make it your business to limit their access to you because being around you is a privilege. You don't get paid on a job unless you work right? No one expects a free paycheck if they haven't clocked in for two weeks. In that same token if a person is not putting in work to respect, love, and support you why are we giving them free paychecks week after week to enjoy the privileges and benefits which is your presence? Exit stage left please, don't even pick up the mic to explain for the 15th time what they should have said/did or shouldn't have. Run as far away from these type of people at Usain Bolt pace as they lack accountability and you don't need this type of headache to teach them how to gain it. You didn't go to college to earn a bachelor's in teaching people how to be a good person 101 nor did you take respect me 200 as an elective. Not your responsibility, sis, so don't make it as such.

Act Like a Black Card, Not a Prepaid One

Have you ever seen those black credit cards individuals with a certain type of credit or wealth have? It's an elite credit card where they pay a yearly fee. It's on some next level Ciara dance move status. It's one of those credit cards that only the elite can obtain. The average old folk can't afford it. I need you to treat yourself like a black card. Meaning everybody doesn't get access to you. Everybody doesn't deserve your kind heart. Everybody doesn't deserve explanations on why you move the way you move. Everyone doesn't deserve to continue to be your friend after they've been everything but a friend to you. They don't deserve to get a thousand chances to be your boyfriend/husband/girlfriend/wife. Elite status! Only the deserving get it. When people have proved they know how to handle the responsibility well they can be granted access. You don't give your black card to people unless they have shown evidence they have good credit and can use responsibly. Meaning you have a good payment history and you are very likely to pay for the bill month after month. I need you to treat people that same way. They have to prove to you they are going to treat you well and continue to show you they're trustworthy of accessing you in any shape form or fashion. If they haven't shown you that I need you to put them on prepaid RushCard status until they show you otherwise. They only get what they put in until they've established better history. Don't put yourself on clearance as you are worth more than you are giving yourself credit for. They're not going to cause you harm mentally or physically moving forward.

Superhero evaluation questions to ask yourself:

- Why is it important for you to know the rationale behind mistreatment? And once you know will it change the fact that you desire to be treated with dignity?

- List out the type of behavior you feel is nonnegotiable and that you can no longer accept?

- What are your steps to take if a person chooses not to honor your request for respect? This may be difficult emotionally to not want to break down the reasons why like a fraction so how will you mentally cope with asking less and taking more action?

Chapter 29

Don't Take It Personal

Superwoman Tana has a coworker that has not liked her since her start date. Her coworker has been blatantly rude Tana can't think of anything she has done to cause the discord at work.

I feel we only take things personally when we question whether what was said or did is true or not. For example, when someone says to you, "You're so dumb," why do you get so offended? You know you're not dumb, but if you're doubting your intellect, you're going to be *very* upset when someone says something like that. We as women must know who we are and what we stand for and we also have to know that sometimes when people say or do things it has nothing to do with us and everything to do with them. Sometimes people are going through something or *wasn't raised right* as my grandma would say (I know yall are sick of hearing about my granny but she was a wise funny woman). They maybe are not a good person and maybe they're just being a crappy person to everybody they encounter, but they didn't singlehandedly pick you out and say, "Hey, let me be horrible to her." They may be nasty to everybody so don't take it personal and know what somebody thinks or feels about you is none of your business. They have a right to have an opinion and you have a right to not listen or agree with their opinion. Let it slide off your back. Definitely easier said than done, but just know what other people do is not because of you. We are being a little selfish when we think people's actions or words have to do with us. Sometimes it has everything to do with the other person and you were just at the wrong place at the wrong time. We are naturally selfish people and we make conscious efforts to be considerate of others. Some people decide they don't want to be considerate and choose to go with their instinct. When these people say or do things that may be hurtful. You must ask yourself are they hitting a nerve because I am unsure of how I view myself? Possibly, but it's definitely not a personal attack against you. Maybe they're just touching on an insecurity by sheer luck. You don't want to set yourself up to suffer for nothing and that's exactly what happens when you take things as a personal attack against you. I need you to write a note on your bathroom mirror or put a daily reminder on your phone to go off at certain time: don't take anything personally today no matter how hard it is. I'm not going to take an offense as an attack on my worth as an individual.

Also, don't look for people to throw you a parade with the marching band every time you do something great. It's just not going to happen. And even if people do celebrate you, sometimes they may not cheer as loud as you think they should. You have to be ok with celebrating your own milestones no matter how big or small they are. A little painful to accept this reality but a hard pill of truth I want you to swallow. It will save you a lot of disappointment and frustration later.

Superhero evaluation questions to ask yourself:

- What are you currently taking personal that you can say is not a reflection of you as a person but the other individual?

- Why does this person's words/actions alter your mood so drastically?

- Do you feel the person's behavior/words are a true representation of your worth or can it be simply the person is self-involved and not thinking about how they affect others?

- What's a committed action/positive stance you are willing to take when people come at you hard so you can remind yourself it's not personal?

Chapter 30

Friends: How Many of Us Have Them?

Superwoman Dani has been "friends" with Cora since the 5th grade. She's borrowed money and hasn't paid her back, ditched her for events for the latest person she is dating, and lately Dani has noticed when she is going through a personal struggle Cora isn't available for her stating she is "busy."

"Friends" is a term loosely used often. I know a relative used to say to me, "That's your associate, baby-not your friend." I would respond by rolling my eyes, thinking she was old school and didn't know what she was talking about. But a few crashes and burns of supposed friendships later, I began to think maybe she was on to something. Sometimes, we are a bit too quick to give the title of "friend" to people who don't deserve it. Ponder on a few questions that will help you discern and evaluate if you really have friends-or just acquaintances:

- Do you feel the friendship is onesided? Meaning one person puts more effort into the relationship than the other?
- Do you feel he/she is a good listener?
- Can you share your goals and dreams with your friend?
- Are your friends motivating and encouraging you? If not, what are they doing? Are they negative, indifferent, or positive when you have conversations regarding something important to you?
- Do you find yourself withholding information due to the fear of what they may say?
- Do your friends' poor decisions ever affect your life?

- Do your friends celebrate your success or diminish your milestones?
- Have your friends broken your trust in a major way-such as lying, stealing, etc.?
- Are your friends people you can learn from? [Are they willing to share information that would benefit you both or are they likely to keep this information for themselves?]

If you had to think hard about many of these questions, maybe it's time to subtract yourself if things aren't adding up. And yes, I know there can be difficulty and awkwardness when looking for new friends. For me it was very easy in college and below to make friends as I was surrounded by peers with similar interests. However once I moved to a new state it became difficult in my 30s to make new friends once I evaluated my old ones and did a little "spring cleaning." It seems most people already have their "crew," so they aren't too messed up about adding anyone new to the mix. The women I encountered seemed laissez-faire to me about phone calls, texts, meet ups, etc. because you are still in the testing-to-be-their-friend process, and if it doesn't work out with you, they have a backup of homegirls they can call. It became a big effort and at times a little disheartening to find people you can be yourself with and keke without judgement when needed. Especially since I consider myself to be an extrovert.

Even more disappointing when you hang out with someone and you realize she/he is just not your type of person. You quickly realize that person is not someone you desire friendship with. However I was diligent about it. I stayed on my course and I was able to find people I'm still friends with now. During this extroverted journey in my late 20's and early 30's, I realized I wouldn't have the same quantity as before, but I would have quality friendships. I thought that because I liked people, I needed many friends. *Wrong!* I don't know why I thought I needed a gang of people, and, to be honest, having so many people in my life who weren't properly vetted in the friend process is probably why I was burned so many times by associates. I can't call them friends because they never truly were. I was a friend to them, and they categorized and treated me like an acquaintance. It used to hurt my feelings something terrible to realize I'd climb a mountain for people who wouldn't round the corner for me. I saw a meme on social media that says you can go to the moon and back for someone and they will have the audacity to say, "I never asked you to." I almost ran around my living room filled with the "fake friend indicator" spirit. That was so on point with me. I had to ask myself what I was going to do about it. I had to change some things. I challenge you to evaluate the people you know and determine whether they deserve their spots in your life. Ask yourself why you have these people around? Is it because they've been your friend since you were in elementary, because you are related, maybe you work together-meaning you've just grown accustomed to them being around-or are they really good to you? I know we sometimes want to cling to familiar people as that's our comfort zone and nothing wrong with that. However, sometimes you have to meet and spend time with friends who can expose you to greater things, new information and potentially a higher level of living. Maybe if you connect with new people you can grow in areas. We all have things we excel in and other areas that need a little fine tuning. Maybe your new friends can help balance you on out. You never know they may be a subject matter expert in that area you aren't too fond of and can help you tap into that potential as well as enhance those, skills and abilities

Choose friends with similar values. Now I'm all about some diversity. But make sure your friends don't have you compromising your character. You want to be able to sleep peacefully at night child! So, make sure these ladies and gents you associate with don't have you negatively influenced, will hold you accountable and pull your collar if you get to cutting up and get beside yourself.

Chapter 31

"Mind Your Business, See" (Will Smith voice)

Superwoman Oasis wants to start an event planning business. Yet she hasn't had time to create a portfolio, website, print business cards, nor advertise her services. Right now she does small events for her family and friends when asked.

We spend 40+ hours a week working for another company. Now while we are compensated for our time being our paychecks, this job just may not be our passion and often we are stuck in the rat race of waiting every two weeks to get paid, feel undervalued, overworked, annoyed by the job and your coworkers, possibly unfulfilled as this job isn't what you enjoy doing. Jet li quoted: You are killing yourself for a company that would replace you within a week if you dropped dead. I don't know about you but that spoke volumes to me because it's so true. We are not irreplaceable career wise. Companies were running smoothly before we were hired on and will function just fine long after we turn in our notice. Yet we often find ourselves so loyal to a company that isn't ours. We fear the unknown of leaving that steady paycheck and guaranteed health benefits. I call it the platinum handcuffs. They give us all these perks in corporate America that we feel we just can't let go of or wonder how we are going to survive without them that it paralyzes us from taking the ultimate leap of faith on ourselves. Occasionally in the millennium generation we do work up the guts to start something part time. There's nothing wrong with having a side hustle. And I know you're thinking well this side hustle doesn't pay all my bills. For now it doesn't but if you consistently spend enough time watering and caring for a plant what does it do: GROW! But you can't plant the seed and expect to eat the fruit in the same day.

Consistently and diligently work on your small business. It was like pulling teeth for me to start my private practice as my "side hustle/small business" because I grew up in lower economic status and I told myself once I finished college I never wanted to be financially unstable, go back to living a certain lifestyle or ever feel uncertain if I had money to eat. I feared making poor financial decisions like people in my family, so I was always overly aware of my finances. With that being said I felt a small business meant an unsteady paycheck and I couldn't have it where I didn't know when and how much I was getting paid because your girl has bills that have to get paid and I didn't want late or lack of payments affecting my credit that I'd worked so hard to build.

However with the convincing of a few mentors I agreed to start my practice (create my LLC) part time in October 2014 and treat it as a second job. I was surprised at how quickly I was able to generate income once I really gave sufficient effort to it. I also was surprised that it wasn't as difficult as I thought to start. By spring 2015 I had steady clientele and enough income to cover my overhead expenses. By 2016 I went from subleasing to leasing my own space. Now in 2019, I'm making plans to walk away from my great paying, benefits having, work at home corporate America job in 2019 and start my practice full time. Now I've had some mishaps that I can tell you about because it wasn't all smooth sailing. However, that's another story for another book that I can now laugh about. But let me tell you it wasn't funny when it happened. However, the good has outweighed the bad of being in business for myself. I'm jumping out the plane at high altitude on my brand. And let me be honest I'm TERRIFIED of taking this risk. Because again there's no min or max of my income.

However I've been taking the strides to pay down/off bills, save money for a rainy day, project monthly income, calculate expenses, etc. . to be prepared for this transition. I had this constant doubt in my head on if I could be successful and really make this work. But I had to ask myself if other people can do it why can't I? What's the difference between them and me? Nothing really if I'm pushing past my emotions and focusing on facts. I truly believe if people stay consistent, put in the hard work necessary, don't give excuses, do not get deterred by their mistakes and give up, anyone has the right and entitlement to success. Yes, girl, even *you*. I had a million reasons why this thing could blow up in my face, but I had to think of a million reasons as to how this could work, too. Oftentimes, we go into "What if it doesn't work?" mode, but we rarely go to into "What if it *does* work?" mode. Using myself for example. I am single with no children. Now is the perfect time for me to take a calculated risk into self-employment. But this window of opportunity won't be here forever because I'm claiming my husband and beautiful chocolate baby boy with curly hair born in the spring. Specific much huh lol. Hey, you have to speak things into existence.

But back to my business. I am going to take the risks. Because if it fails, I can always go back to work for someone else's company. Jobs don't stop needing to be filled, especially in major cities such as Dallas with a booming job market. But I can't always have the option to work for myself. Also think about big companies you know. I'm sure when they started the owners worked for other companies as they had personal bills and obligations as well. But if they didn't take that risk and branch out independently, they wouldn't be the powerhouse they are now. Possibly when you have a chance look up Google, Apple, Facebook and amazon's beginnings online. These people didn't wake up and become billion-dollar corporations in a single day. They started small but planned for big. So, maybe ask yourself can you put five minutes a day, that's right just five minutes a day into your business. That's 35 minutes a week, 1,820 minutes within a year, which is roughly 30 hours. Imagine what you could accomplish with 30 hours of straight work!! Now I'm not talking about the work where you get distracted and take a restroom break, go eat, talk on the phone, etc. . I'm talking about all these minutes are put into your baby, your brand, your business. Now if you have more time great go for it. The five minutes isn't set in stone. I am suggesting trying to keep it small initially so it's feasible because again I know we are all are very busy ladies. Point is put just as much if not more energy into something you have ownership in and can benefit from vs putting all your eggs into the one basket of someone else's company. You may get a raise, promotion, and occasional bonus, but at the end of the day, you don't own that company-so you won't see the all the fruits of your labor working for someone else all your life. Now let me be clear. There is nothing wrong with working for an employer if you have no desire for self-employment because I am aware this option is not everyone's calling. If you desire to work for a great company there are continuing educations, certifications or promotions you can work for. This is merely a wakeup call for those who do desire self-employment. I need you to really put pedal to the medal and give it one hundred percent not fifty percent. Don't have your employer as your safety crutch when you know your business could be booming. If you are a bit overwhelmed about how to proceed check into your local small business development center. Most offer free classes and/or consultative services to help point you in the right direction. Do you have any family members who own a business? Even if it's a totally different industry it still doesn't hurt to have a conversation with them to see how they kept the lights on and give you tips.

Superhero evaluation questions to ask yourself:

- Have you considered partnering with someone? Maybe you'd feel more comfortable making this move if you had another person to depend on with the semantics.

- I would say write down your ultimate goal, a soft timeframe (as things don't always go as we planned) what steps can you take to make this a reality within one month, three months, six months and one year.

- Do you have a certain profit margin you are trying to meet in a certain timeframe?

- Can you put a reminder on your phone/calendar to track your progress?

Chapter 32

Focus on Your Coin, Honey!

Superwoman Phoenix is head over her heels in credit card debt as she had a weakness for a good sale. However she wants to be more financially stable to purchase a home in the next 2 years

Invest in yourself. Have you always wanted to earn your degree, take that trip to Dubai, learn how to play the guitar or enroll in classes to brush up on some professional skills to take your career to the next level? Sometimes, spending a little money now can make you a lot of money later. But it doesn't always have to be financial to be a great investment. Even though a yoga or photography class might not help you earn more income, the happiness or health benefits it brings could be worth more than the one percent interest you're earning in a savings account.

Invest more for retirement. Even though it seems far away it eventually will come.

Prioritize early on your 401k/retirement, even if you start small and increase your contributions incrementally. If you have access to an employer-sponsored retirement plan, aim to contribute at least enough to recoup any company match to start. No 401(k)? Open an Individual Retirement Account (IRA) with your bank and you can sock away up to five hundred dollars per year.

Do you have life insurance? Nothing worse than your family trying to throw a fish fry together to pay Browns funeral home since you didn't plan. Don't be that family member putting others in a bind.

Do you have a will? Who's getting your Destiny's Child CDs and that one pair of red bottoms? And I know you are probably thinking, "Wills are for senior citizens." *Wrong.* Everyone who has assets or needs one-and if you don't have assets, maybe it's time to consider acquiring some. It's cool to look good with the bundles, clothes, and car, but let's look good in our long-term assets, as well.

Invest for medium-term goals, too

From buying a home to starting a side business, you probably have some mid-term financial goals in mind. You'll get there a lot faster by letting your money start growing early. Ensure your investments match your risk tolerance and timeline. Generally, the more time you have before you need the money, the more you can invest in stocks versus, say, bonds.

Pay off expensive debt. Start a debt snowball to see how this can be started. Like inflation, debt works against our efforts to build wealth. The more high-interest debt you carry, the harder it is to boost your net worth—making paying down that debt faster a worthy use of extra cash. Start with expensive debt with high interest rates (think: credit cards, auto loans and personal loans) before moving on to mortgages and student loans. Don't forget that paying off debt means you're saving on debt and interest payments—so you're freeing up even more money you can use to work for you. When I did my debt snowball, I realized I was paying $6.02 a day in interest on my student loans. That's a ridiculous amount of money to waste. Seeing this amount was the motivation I needed to start paying extra on my principle. Ask yourself is there any way you can get more involved with your money? If you don't know where to start maybe see if you can speak to a financial advisor for assistance. If you work for a fortune 500 company utilize your Employee Assistance Program for a free 30 minute consultation with a financial advisor if offered.

Chapter 33

Student Loans Affect My Ability to Be Bad and Boujee…

I owe the equivalent of what a trap house costs in student loan payments. Like seriously I do!! Now granted I have a master's degree and am a few classes into my doctorate, but I still cringe every month when they take that car note from my banking account which is my student loan payment. I've seen people stunting hard in undergrad with the new car, clothes, and eating steak/lobster for breakfast. Everyone was so happy after the second week of school when that refund check touched their hands. But I think we forget at 18 years of age that we have to pay it back when we're 30. Whether a person has a trade or degree those student loans are like a dark cloud hanging over your head. Some cannot afford the payment and often do the "I have six dependents" trick-dog and cat included-to get that low monthly payment. I understand why people avoid the payment because we all have other bills that we deem more important. We can't put it off forever-though we wish we could click our magic Wizard of Oz Dorothy shoes, they'd disappear, and you'd be back at your momma's house debt free. Maybe we should take a look at how to bring the debt down or eliminate it once and for all; because if you don't pay, they can eventually garnish your wages. Plus, if you take a close look at your statement you could be wasting $100-200 a month just in accruing interest. So, now that we are full-fledged adulting and realize you and Sallie Mae may go together for life if you don't take action. What is a realistic solution?

If you work in a public service field such as teaching, firefighter, nonprofit agency, government/state employee, police officer etc. if you make 10 years of payment the rest will be forgiven so call your loan carrier and ask if you make those consecutive 120 payments will they forgive the other 120. https://studentloanhero.com/featured/public-service-loan-forgiveness-do-you-qualify/ or https://studentaid.ed.gov/sa/repay-loans/forgiveness-cancellation/public-service

If your interest rates are ridiculous, have you considered refinancing? I didn't know you could refinance your student loans, but I eventually refinanced mine through Sofi to a 10 year, my interest rate dropped 2% and I saved thousands in the long run. Now, FYI-if you refinance it turns into a private loan and you can no longer qualify for the loan forgiveness mentioned above.

Some employers offer a loan repayment so possibly check into that, especially if you are in or were in the military. You can see if you work for your company for so long how much will they apply towards your loan. https://www.opm.gov/policy-data-oversight/pay-leave/student-loan-repayment/

Make sure there are no prepayment penalties if you make extra payments with your current loan provider to pay it off early. Some do have this as they want to get you on the interest.

If you are back in school, lost your job, are having financial difficulties, etc., then maybe consider deferment/forbearance https://studentaid.ed.gov/sa/repay-loans/deferment-forbearance

If you are receiving SSI/SSDI you may can have your loans discharged https://studentaid.ed.gov/sa/repay-loans/forgiveness-cancellation/disability-discharge

If you've filed bankruptcy, you may can qualify for a discharge https://studentaid.ed.gov/sa/repay-loans/forgiveness-cancellation/bankruptcy

Other ways to discharge a loan: you didn't receive your refund, attended a Corinthian college, etc., https://studentaid.ed.gov/sa/repay-loans/forgiveness-cancellation

Instead of not paying, why not ask your current loan carrier what payment plans they offer: 10, 15, 20, 25, or 30 year installment plan. Maybe you can reach out for a more realistic payment plan you can afford verses going with the flow of the current one. If you have more than one loan have you considered consolidating for one payment to help your pockets and having a better chance of paying down the principle?

Avoid the scams. A lot of companies pretend to help you eliminate debt but usually are rip offs so make sure you are educated on what's legit http://clark.com/personal-finance-credit/beware-student-loan-debt-payment-scams/

Educate your kids and family members on student loan debt so they can avoid it if possible and teach them how to pay for college or trade school with alternative methods. If money is funny, then avoid colleges like the University of Phoenix, fancy cosmetology programs, and other online schools as they are significantly more expensive. I'd say a community college or small cosmetology program would be your best bet as it's affordable and most credits transfer to major universities later and eventually, you get the same state licenses once you're done. Help them apply for FAFSA so they can qualify for grants https://fafsa.ed.gov/, see if they can obtain work study. Maybe check out scholarship sites such as:

- Collegeboard.org
- Fastweb.com
- Niche.com (formerly College Prowler)
- Moolahspot.com

Point is, you don't want to be 65 still having anniversaries with Sallie Mae.

Superhero evaluation questions to ask yourself:

- Are you on top of your student loan payments?

- You can't claim to be bad and boujee if you owe the folks their coins. What are you willing to do to get a handle on your loans?

Chapter 34

Is My Clock Broken, Or Do I Need Some New Batteries?

Superwoman Urvi is 38 and desperately wants to be married. She was content with her single life until last year she attend 3 weddings, 4 baby showers and 7 kids birthday parties/baby christenings. Now she is hyper aware of her biological clock.

Are you really ready to be married and have kids or do you feel like because you are at a certain age, many of your friends or family members are doing these things, you are tired of getting asked at the company picnic if you're dating anyone and you would love to have a plus one to an event versus going solo? If I had to answer the question for you probably not. It's no different from you seeing the weight loss commercials and you starting to think you're overweight and now for the first time in your life you want to master the gym. When 2 minutes ago you thought you were slim thick and loved how you looked in your maxi dress. Whatever it is that you consume usually persuades you to feel or act a certain way. Seeing image after image of the family that America projects you can have if you just follow the rules of going to college, attend church, act lady like and whatever else out of date standards your mind can come up with you'll be there by age 32. Now all these reasons are challenging and can sometimes toy with her mental if it hasn't happened yet. But this doesn't necessarily mean it's our timing for these things. I want you to honestly ask yourself If no one ever asked you about it, made you feel less than at family functions, there was no 35 and under gynecologist conversation scare, you didn't see the picture perfect family photos on social media and do a compare and contrast, and/or society wasn't pushing the agenda down our throat, would you still feel the same pressure to have these things like yesterday? Would it still hold as much importance?

Being in the dating scene is like being in the wilderness: you're bound to get some wild animals who are untrained and ready to attack their prey. But seriously, I am aware that dating can be hard and exhausting. It can be frustrating, so when you finally do meet someone that you make a connection with and they treat you halfway decently, you get excited, like: "Yes! I can get out of the wilderness for a while!" You may have a little bit of a routine going on with him or her. You're glad to have someone to cuddle with at night-whatever makes your toes curl, child. Free facts for when you get in this stage, though: don't alter your whole life routine for this person. (For example, instead of working out three times a week, now you skip gym days so you can spend time with this special person, or instead of hanging out with your girlfriends, you cancel so you can be with "boo thang.") The problem with this is, what happens in the worst-case scenario where you guys break up? Then your whole life has been flipped upside down and you don't know what to do with yourself now that you can't orbit around this person thus making the break up seem detrimental. It makes it ten times harder to let go of the relationship because he or she's been implemented into every aspect of your life. Which is turn makes you feel as though your clock is ticking ever so loudly each and every second of the day. It's pressure we don't need. Know that your clock is fine, and it doesn't need to be touched once set because I think it forces you to be in the moment and live your life verses focusing on the future and not being content on all the things you can be thankful for. I don't care how much you think, wish, or dream about it you cannot set the clock back so why not enjoy the seconds while they are happening verse focusing on the next hour?

Chapter 35

Single as A Dollar Bill: Does Singleness=Mental Illness?

There is no blueprint for singleness. There's a YouTube video circulating of a man saying something is wrong with a woman over thirty who hasn't been married with children. Being that I'm over thirty and am not married with children I found it quite offensive. I often have encountered this stereotype when approached by men, family and/or people I don't know who feel the need to ask, "Do you even want children?" As though I have three heads because it hasn't happened yet, and I should just take the first man coming my way and be in an unhappy marriage to appease them vs having standards. How dare me have values and expectations of my mate right?! Is it really their business to ask me such a personal question and something is so horrifically wrong with me because I haven't marked this off my to do list yet? Is there a rule that I must have a $60 marriage certificate and $700-$1,000 monthly day care bill since we know these naysayers aren't going to help with any babysitting nor contribute to any marriage counseling if it goes south? Yet again it makes them feel better to know I'm not "crazy" and am someone's wife and mother like there aren't wives and parents who aren't crazy as a Betsy bug walking around right now doing the most(yea I know that's country but oh well lol). Hmmm, guess I'm assumed to be less of a woman because I'm not in the married category, NOT!!!

Many people share the guy mentioned above idiotic stance for women like you and I. What I don't understand is when it became such a bad thing to do things the way I see fit? Meaning what works for me. Why are we single ladies getting punished and looked down upon for saying Hey I believe in the free birth control (thanks Obama) and want to wait till marriage to have children vs having them out of wedlock and possibly with multiple people (no judgment or negativity intended if you are in this category because I know a lot of dope single mothers, heck my mom had to become one post-divorce), I want to finish school and get my career going before focusing on my husband and children, I want to travel the world carefree which requires money, I don't want to rush into a lifelong commitment until I know it's feels right with the right person in my own opinion not yours as we will be in this thing forever and I'm responsible enough and ready to be a good wife, I want to be financially stable to care for my children etc. . I'm lost on why it automatically means something is wrong with the woman and her mental stability vs her being sane enough to know herself and what she can and can't handle. Personally, I've enjoyed going to college, traveling the world, saving money, and growing the heck up because your girl was real immature in her teens/early 20's and I would hate to have a child seeing some of those behaviors and be anybody's misses while being in that immature mindset. So, I think my 30's is a better time for me as I understand the responsibility and the importance of being a wife and mother as well as I can dedicate more time to both as I've lived a little and do not feel as though I'd be missing out on anything (I know people who had children early and now are big time partying still, in the college parties/clubs because they couldn't do so ten years ago). I just think it's a slap in the face to a woman who's made a conscious effort to be responsible enough to know herself for anyone to frown upon her for doing so but be perfectly fine with a woman who's maybe not been as responsible. Just seems a$$ backwards to me and it makes a woman feel as though one is degrading her while in the same breath praising another when maybe people should just ZIP IT and not say anything because who are they to tell someone else what's right and wrong for them. They wouldn't want anyone to stereotype them regarding race, religion, sexuality, economic status, political stance, etc. So, why in turn would you stereotype a woman without a husband or children?!?!?! How would you feel if you met someone and they were psychoanalyzing you trying to figure out what's wrong with you when they don't know you only to appease the image they have in their head for you?! Wouldn't feel so good huh? To me it just puts pressure on women to marry prematurely and I feel that contributes to the ever growing divorce rate as some women become so focused on getting married and having babies to conform to what is shoved down their throats vs seeing if this person is really a good fit for them long term.

A good friend of mine posted a response on Facebook and I couldn't agree more:

Not every woman has had the opportunity to get married by her early 30's.

Not every woman is ok with having children out of wedlock…which is how a lot of people end up with children before their 30's.

Not every woman makes her relationship status the center of her life or the baseline for how "successful" or "normal" she is.

This isn't 1946 and having a husband is not necessary for a lot of women to have financial security…which was a key motivator for past generations of women to get married and *stay* married to people who didn't treat them well.

A lot of the same men who will ask what's "wrong" with you for being single at 33 will have two roommates, three baby mamas, and a 234 credit score. Don't let it stress you out, ladies.

Can we start learning to live and let live *without* judging or wanting people to conform to your beliefs and values?! Ladies it's ok to tell people the question is too intrusive, it's none of their business and to live your best single life. This is the year we stop awkwardly answering and smiling through discomfort, attempting to be polite. This is the year we ask/tell people how these questions/comments make us feel and ask them not to ask and remind them this is a conversation you don't feel comfortable having.

Chapter 36

Waiting to Get Picked Up at The Grocery Store

Superwoman Petra is a 36 year old single female. She works an average of 55-60 hours a week on the job. She spends her off days catching up on sleep and/or running errands. She desires to have companionship and is a bit envious of her friends whom are married and/or have children.

You want to get married or have a significant other before your gray hairs do the most, but you don't go out so how does that work in that pretty little head of yours? Make it make sense to me! Do we as women really think the stars will align just right on our mac slayed to capacity faces and our future Mr. (insert your last name) will see you picking up those fresh grapes in your FashionNova maxi dress at your local suburban neighborhood Walmart with a population of -8.983% single people and 37.2% families, and say,"Yep, that's wifey right there?" It just doesn't work that way, sistahs, sorry-well, unless you're in a dumb Tyler Perry movie…Now I'm pretty sure if you're in your late 20's to early 40's, you're more than likely past that "Ladies get in free before 11" and "$5 Crown and down that ends at 7pm" regular happy hour crowd (don't judge my former life). We can more than likely find you on your couch, with a hair bonnet on, watching Golden Girls reruns on Friday nights or helping your 39th homegirl plan a bridal shower/baby shower/kids birthday party. I get it, the night life and all that jazz is not your thing anymore. But now that you aren't party chasing and prefer a quieter scene these days the question is how do you meet someone? If your week consists of working, running errands and family time then do you expect the person of your dreams to knock on your front door and propose? Now unless you happen to have a one in three million chance of a fine amazon prime delivery guy/girl giving you a package sistah girl you have to get out the house and make yourself available. So, what are your options as you bravely jump into the wilderness of dating, as let's be honest it's a jungle in these single streets!!

Accept invitations. If you want to meet new people, don't turn down all invitations to social events that don't involve your bestie/favorite cousin. Even if you think the event might not be your "thing," and you really want to catch that rerun of Living Single that you've seen 34,205 times, take a chance and go anyway. You never know who you'll meet or what connections you might make. You can always leave if you're having a bad time, but if you don't go, you'll never know the possibilities.

I like the old saying: Don't poop where you eat (PG-13 version), so I can't get down with dating coworkers. However, if you work for a major company and see a cutie in another department, you guys have different work schedules, or you know you won't be there too much longer, then YOLO if he/she asks you to lunch!

Superhero evaluation questions to ask yourself:

1. Take your book, computer or iPad to a coffee house vs reading at home. Strike up a conversation with the person at the table next to you. You never know who you might meet and may enjoy!

2. Travel the world or at least see some other states besides the ones within driving distance and ask yourself are you open to long distance dating. Hey don't knock it till you try it. I know some married couples right now that started off in different states and other countries for that matter so it can happen to you, yep, you as well.

3. There's online dating. I know child I know (closes eyes for a moment of silence), you are so tired of fishing in that Flint contaminated sea POF (*Plenty of Fish*) and you've heard the horror story dates from hell. But everyone on there isn't lying about who they are, trying to hook up after the second text or has a gold tooth. For every 20 weirdos, I'm sure one is "normal" and doesn't have a foot fetish. Sometimes you can meet decent people and even if it doesn't pan out to a relationship you may add another good homeboy to the list to help you move or kill that mouse that came in your home. You just have to sort through the riff raff (and if they do have that foot fetish, then politely decline unless you're into that *blank stare*), but the upside of online dating is you have access to *many* more people in a shorter period of time than in person. I'm living proof. I had percolator low expectations for online dating, but I just celebrated a year of dating current bae and we met on

a free online dating app so if it can happen to me it can happen to you.

4. Meetup.com. If you have something that lights your fire join a meetup group and you'll find likeminded people who share your interests and can have some good old-fashioned fun. Scroll through the various events in your city to find something of interest and see what's available. I've found book clubs (superwoman redefined would be a great suggestion lol), networking groups, and social groups through Meetup.

5. Well there's church. You could be one of the fifty women in a singles group vying for the attention of that one man that attended with his too tight khakis. Just kidding, but to be honest I've heard many friends say they enjoy the single events their church has and met some great people they now call friends.

6. Go to seminars, book signings, or speaking events. Yelp always has a schedule for festivals, cultural and free events in your area. LinkedIn has business networking events and your local chamber of commerce may meet regularly. Also, Toastmasters is a good club to help you learn to be a better public speaker and meet other professionals.

7. Group runs/group workouts such as Herbalife sports clubs (I'm the Herbalife plug btw so holla atcha girl https://www.goherbalife.com/ashleyhence/en-US please don't judge my grinding spirit to secure the coin legally lol) may be a good way to see some eye candy. You may meet that former college running back 10 minutes past his

prime but still trying to preserve his sexy. Also swing out lessons are a nice way to bust a move and get up close and personal for some good clean fun.

8. Get a part time job as a hostess, tour guide, bartender, waitress something that allows you to be in a social environment a few hours a week and a chance to connect with other people.

9. When's the last time you've been to your local farmers market or went to a new restaurant/bar in your town. Try a spot totally different from your norm: take a hike, art class, fish, make jewelry, go horse riding, a Segway tour, visit a museum, take a computer class, jazz club, poetry lounge, river rafting-ok wait can you swim? If not scratch that idea lol.

10. Do you know your neighbors? Now again I personally don't poop where I eat but maybe having a cute lil themed social and inviting some known and unknown peeps to the soiree similar to a fresh prince party, wear what you feel costume, turtle necks and tequila, murder mystery plot, game of thrones, etc. . My lil weird imagination is running wild but do you boo boo on a fun night with some inexpensive food and drinks at your apartments open area/pool.

11. Now it took me awhile to get used to this one but what if people want to introduce you to someone, will you let them? We all have somebody in our life (usually an older woman who doesn't have a good eye for what handsome really means) screaming I have the perfect person for you

even if they aren't the perfect person. But what if you did have a homegirl/boy that did know your taste and would merely introduce, not hook up, introduce you to a possible suitor. Would you be open to this?

I'm not saying live your life based on your relationship status or go with the expectation every social outing will end with a love connection. Point is, people must know your cute, smart, funny, awesome self is available-and they can't know that if you're on "work, drive home, repeat" mode. Now I'm by no means implying be single and desperate I'm just saying when a new product hits the market, how does the company let people know it's ready for purchase: they advertise! So, get out the house! No one is going to hit on you in your living room. Well maybe they will if again the UPS worker is bold, but why not increase those chances of getting hit on if you are out enjoying life doing tons of other stuff.

What say ye ladies. Do you think your current lifestyle lets others know you are single and ready to mingle? If not, how can you make yourself more available?

Chapter 37

Keep It Simple

We get so caught up with work, school, parenting, deadlines, trying to make time for family and friends, socializing, and keeping our bodies tight that it feels like we are on a never-ending "to do" list. It can be complicated as well as overwhelming. Sometimes, it's refreshing to do simple things to remind us that life isn't so bad. Sometimes, you have to remind yourself, *It's a bad day/week, but not a bad life.* When is the last time you spread a blanket out in your backyard and stared at the stars? The other day, I played hide and seek with my four- and two-year-old little cousins. I hadn't done so since I was a child. It was surprisingly fun. The game required no technology, money, or even lots of effort- it was just entertaining for them and me. Their little laughs just filled my heart. I challenge you to consider maybe just going back to the basics. I'm talking about the peanut butter and jelly sandwich vs. the gourmet meals. I'm talking about having a good conversation with somebody and leaving the phones at home or in the car so you can give that person your undivided attention. I mean calling someone or going to their house rather than sending them a message on social media and checking off your mental "kept in touch" list. I mean maybe going to see somebody and catching a couch versus checking into a five-star hotel. Sometimes, I feel we get beside ourselves and think we need so much. Think back to before we had all the materialistic things. We were able to be happy with so little in our younger years.

I challenge you to find something to do or a place to go that makes you simplistically happy. *Only you*. Now, I'm not saying go online and start trying to plan that vacation to the beach outside of your budget. *Keep it simple.* Something that you can do in an afternoon, or even after work, that may just take an hour or two out of your day. (Twenty years ago, I believe we did things like this more because there was no technology like there is now. Today, if we're not checking boxes off our daily lists, we're probably interacting on social media or browsing for something to purchase online for temporary joy). This should not require much thought or effort. It can be any task or place that allows you to look out at the world with a smile which you may not do as often anymore. Like my playing hide and seek, I basically want you to try and be a kid again. Find or create a place in your life where you don't have to stress or worry. Just look for your next place or thing to pour your energy into for enjoyment. Just for one hour. Go!

Superhero evaluation questions to ask yourself:

- What inspired you today?

- What are you thankful for today?

- What was the best part of your day?

- Who did you enjoy talking to today?

Chapter 38

To-Go Plate: Last Minute Take-aways

1. If you avoid conflict to keep the peace you start a war inside of yourself

2. Train your mind to be stronger than your feelings. We can say all day long how we feel about something, but does it really make it true? Perception and reality are two different things: how you feel about something vs. what it really is. Do you have evidence to support those insecurities you're caring around everyday?

3. Trust your own intuition-don't borrow someone else's like a cup of sugar. When something is nagging at you, your first thought is usually right. Trust your gut, sis. Most times, there is a reason you are thinking and feeling a certain way.

4. Everybody's fighting a battle we are just not quite sure what the title of theirs is verses knowing your own.

5. Even Salt Looks Like Sugar-Sometimes when you think you losing you are winning and sometimes when you think you are winning you are losing. Just because something looks good doesn't mean it's actually good for you. My grandma used to tell me even salt looks like sugar. You know Jill Scott has a song titled Fools gold, listen to it when you have a chance. Something may not be the real deal. We get so caught up on what things look like that we don't take the time to figure out what it really is. Don't get so caught up on how people think you are, what you should be, or what you think other people have going on. Don't get so caught up on the

image. Actually get caught up in being the person you want to be.

6. *It is what it is.* This is the statement you have to throw out when you waiver on your feelings because you don't want to hurt someone else's, your nice cup runneth over, to keep the peace, someone makes you feel guilty and/or tell you what you should or shouldn't feel, it goes against the masses. Just remember you aren't responsible for anyone's peace except your own, so the final equation is if there's only one gold trophy, you will take it-and the other person is responsible for figuring out what they need to do to find their peace.

7. *Where'd I place my instructions?* Don't you wish life came with a table of contents that you could look up the page you need to turn to help you get through life's hurdle? Like an encyclopedia you could reference to avoid life's mess up. I know you are sitting there nodding your head. Me to girl, me too. I wish I had one for that time I opened a credit card freshman year so I could get a free t-shirt and pizza. I maxed that thing out to the $1,000 limit so fast. Lesson learned when I struggled to pay it off on my $7. 25 an hour salary. Tragic I know. But I did and lived to tell the tale laughing and shaking my head. There is no instruction manual to life. We are all taking it day by day figuring out what makes us happy.

8. We evolve, our needs change. So, if you make a mistake and have to start over don't pull a Mr. West on us. Just know everyone around you is just as clueless at times. Some are just better actors and can disguise their uncertainties better.

9. Don't mistake a person's cover up performance as confidence and knowledge. Maybe transparency isn't their thing.

10. People can't step on your toes and tell you how loud to say, "Ouch!" When they offend or hurt you they don't own the rights to tell you how to heal and deal with the offense(s) as if they hadn't done anything you wouldn't be reacting at all.

11. No more getting anxiety thinking about future, goals, what ifs etc. that you can't enjoy my right now. Let's focus on our journeys vs the destinations this year

12. Stop setting yourself on fire to make someone else warm- Don't do things you're uncomfortable with. You will either regret it later or resent the person you help when they don't stick their neck out for you the same way.

13. *Check for one please.* Date yourself. Until Mr./Mrs. Right finds you, take yourself out. Don't wait until you get a "bae" to decide to try new things. Buy yourself a "just because" gift if it's within your budget, try new restaurants with friends and family, remind yourself that your butt looks good in those jeans and your twist out/make up is popping. Get into dating yourself so you aren't so starved for attention you start putting yourself on clearance taking discounts on what's romantically acceptable.

14. Don't borrow any problems. When you land at an airport, you go to the baggage claim to wait for your luggage. Are you getting your luggage as well as others'? Sounds like a silly question, right? Of course, you are getting your luggage only. However, in life we often find ourselves trying to take

on other people's thoughts and feelings, fix things for them, or worry about how things affect them. That's not your bag, sweetie. Only get what has your name on the tag as you are responsible for only one person, *yourself*. Now I'm not implying that you should never have empathy nor help anyone. I'm just stating live for today and only help within your means. If you find it's beyond your scope, point that person in the right direction toward resources and leave it up to them to take the initiative to help themselves.

15. The grass definitely looks greener on the other side over there, but the question is: Who's doing the yard work? I know we've heard the clichés: *you shouldn't compare yourself to others* and *you've got to run your own race*, but sometimes doesn't that person's life look so awesome? The part I think we forget is what they have to do to maintain that lifestyle. Ask yourself whether you'd be willing to go through what they did to get or keep it? We compare our grind to other people's shine-but never our sacrifices to their sacrifices as we don't know what theirs are. Comparison will creep into your mind from time-to-time, but make sure you are comparing an apple to an apple. Look at the whole picture-not just their best and your worst. I'd even challenge you to be bold enough to ask that person the pros and cons of the thing(s) you are envying. You may be surprised to learn their perception of the lifestyle you are secretly wishing for. We don't have all the information to make a true analysis as we have all our behind the scene information compared to others highlight reel.

16. Never stop asking for help. It doesn't matter if you've asked ten people and they didn't take you seriously. It doesn't matter if they brushed you off, told you not to feel a certain

way, or gave you bad advice. Keep asking until you get the help you need.

17. It's awesome to finally have that "good job" post-college where you work limited weekends, have a salary/401k, and can wear your big girl clothes rather than a uniform. So, I get it-you want to keep your current lifestyle because maybe you weren't born with a silver spoon in your mouth. But don't let the job equate to your worth and value as a person. Make your money to take care of your personal responsibilities, but if the job becomes the primary focus of your life, then maybe evaluate why it is so important to you outside of the money. Do you have to work so many hours? If you didn't have your job, would you have an identity? Do you put things like working overtime before any and everything? If so, can this be modified? Are you willing to do so and how?

18. Some people will hurt you and then act like you hurt them. People are going to learn that they can't say whatever they want to, claim it was a joke, you're taking it the wrong way or being sensitive. *Nah playa, you meant what you said. That 'lol' at the end was a halfhearted attempt to make it sting a little less.* Well, you are not here for their comedic relief, nor did you volunteer to be roasted. Let's create a new rule to prevent these problems: *Don't joke around me and I won't take it the wrong way-how about that!*

19. Ask yourself: *If I don't deserve it, then who does?* Have you ever had that feeling where you question whether you are deserving or worthy of something? If you're putting in all the blood, sweat, tears and sacrificing to make things play out, then why would anyone else besides you deserve the

rewards? It doesn't make sense to me that we question whether we deserve something we worked hard, sacrificed and dedicated so much toward, and when we finally get the pot of gold at the end of the rainbow, we don't know what to do with it and want to give it back. *"Tast[ing] the Rainbow"* is what we will be doing moving forward. It's a nonnegotiable Ashleyism that has been signed, voted on, and accepted into your personal bylaws. Not up for discussion. Bloop.

20. Get out of your feelings. Ain't nothing there but insecurities.

21. You're a beautiful mess, sweetie. Own it. The gag? So is everyone else. So, go out there and live your best life. You deserve every good thing that comes your way-whether you feel like it some days or not.

22. Learn to take a compliment. Just say, "Thank you," and smile. Nothing else needed.

23. How do you want to be? Figure out how to measure that rather than measuring what you can accomplish.

24. You can have a bad day/week, but that doesn't mean you have a bad life.

25. Don't let the $15K you can't afford to waste make you think your natural body isn't attractive.

26. Selfishness and self-care are not synonymous

27. Turn your messes into messages.

28. How you do one thing is how you do everything.

29. It's ok to only accept love in the way you love. You don't have to settle for mediocrity.

30. Daily reminder: I am amazing, I can do anything, positivity is a choice, I am prepared to succeed

Ashley Hence, LPC-S, CRC, NCC

Ashley Hence is a Licensed Professional Counselor in the state of Texas. She is a member of Zeta Phi Beta Sorority, Inc. Ashley thoroughly enjoys reading and is overly excited to put on her published author hat. A southern girl at heart, this Pine Bluff, Arkansas native has an affinity for sweet tea, soul food, and being on her dad's land hearing no traffic. When she isn't running her private practice in Dallas, she enjoys traveling, spending time with the love of her life (her very spoiled niece, Cailyn), and attending neo-soul concerts.

- Website www.hencecounseling.com
- Facebook https://www.facebook.com/hencecoun/
- Email hencecounseling@gmail.com
- Twitter/Instagram hencecounseling

Made in the USA
Middletown, DE
23 March 2019